Sierra Leone beyond the Lomé Peace Accord

Edited by Marda Mustapha
and Joseph J. Bangura

SIERRA LEONE BEYOND THE LOMÉ PEACE ACCORD
Copyright © Marda Mustapha and Joseph J. Bangura, 2010.

First published in 2010 by PALGRAVE MACMILLAN® in the United States—a division of St. Martin's Press LLC, 175 Fifth Avenue, New York, NY 10010.

Where this book is distributed in the UK, Europe, and the rest of the world, this is by Palgrave Macmillan, a division of Macmillan Publishers Limited, registered in England, company number 785998, of Houndmills, Basingstoke, Hampshire RG21 6XS.

Palgrave Macmillan is the global academic imprint of the above companies and has companies and representatives throughout the world.

Palgrave® and Macmillan® are registered trademarks in the United States, the United Kingdom, Europe and other countries.

ISBN: 978-0-230-10285-9

Library of Congress Cataloging-in-Publication Data is available from the Library of Congress.

A catalogue record of the book is available from the British Library.

Design by Scribe Inc.

First edition: August 2010

10 9 8 7 6 5 4 3 2 1

Printed in the United States of America.

To Hajaratu Yabome, Joseph, Josratu, Jaribu, Jabari;

to Eric and Doris Mustapha for their sacrifice;

and to the memory of Abdul Nafieu Mustapha and the victims and survivors of the Sierra Leone Civil War

Contents

Acknowledgments

The idea of writing a book on postwar Sierra Leone was born at an annual meeting of the African Studies Association (ASA) in San Francisco in 2006. The editors mulled the notion over dinner, and the idea blossomed as a possibility when we put out the call for papers via e-mail. Except for one negative response, we received positive reaction from scholars across the globe. It is fascinating to note that we do not know some of the great contributors to this volume personally, yet we communicated regularly via e-mail. Our thanks go to this remarkable crop of distinguished scholars for their trenchant contributions and blazing, sagacious insights.

Obviously, the book could not have come to fruition without the help, nudging, and encouragement from a number of colleagues. At Kalamazoo College, Joseph would like to thank Michael A. McDonald, Ahmed Hussen, Kiran Cunningham, Charlene Boyer Lewis and members of the history department. At the College of Saint Rose, Marda would like to thank Jenise Depinto, Keith Haynes, and Carl Swidorsky; and, at Northern Arizona University, Carol Thompson.

We would also like to thank family members for creating the imperative, space, and inspiration to undertake such a prodigious task: Hajaratu Yabome Jusuf Bangura, Joseph, Josratu, Jaribu, Jabari and Rahman Mustapha Bangura; Catherine Laverley, Eric Mustapha Jr., Eleanor Michael and Andrew Pessima, Francis and Emily Baion, Dorica Richter, Momoh, Mamie-Kema, Torlo, Pitchounette, Erica, Sharron, Nevylle, and Eric III.

Finally, our special thanks go to Laura E. Lancaster, editorial assistant at Palgrave Macmillan, for her patience and support. We thank Professor Cecil Blake for serving as discussant on the ASA panel that set the stage for the writing of this book. We also thank Abioseh Porter and Onipede Hollist for their invaluable service, and the anonymous readers for their critical comments on the manuscript.

Prologue

I came to this land of
Kutuje
To see for myself
The truth of the
Rumoured wailings.

—*Ola Rotimi, The Gods Are Not to Blame*

The rock we pound our clothes on
by the waterside
will cleanse our soul at dawn
For last night
at Dante's peak
up against the Iroko tree
we witnessed the red hot lava gushing upwards,
after we waved our white cloths for peace
after the marauders and the plunderers
had ransacked and pillaged our village paths
We faded away, unhurriedly
But we came back after the storm
after the swarming bees had drifted away
to drink lemongrass, tea-bush
and ginger beer

—*Ahmed Koroma, "Limbo of the Patriarchs"*

Introduction

Marda Mustapha and Joseph J. Bangura

The 1999 Lomé Peace Accord, signed between the warring factions in the civil war in Sierra Leone, marked an important turning point in one of the most brutal wars Africa witnessed in the 1990s. Like most peace accords, the Lomé Peace Accord was imperfect and all but fell apart in 2000 after the rebel leader Foday Sankoh attempted to attack and take over the capital city, Freetown. The series of events that ensued prompted some scholars to argue that the accord was a failure (Abraham 2001, 2003; Francis 2000; Adebajo 2002; Reno 2000; Alao and Ero 2001; Bangura 2000). Though imperfect with some aspects of the accord collapsing, substantial aspects of the accord were maintained and implemented, and have contributed immensely to the tenuous peace and challenges that currently obtain in Sierra Leone. We argue that the Lomé Peace Accord played a significant role in the cessation of major combat operations, the subsequent achievement of negative peace, and the creation of institutions and regimes with far-reaching implications, both for Sierra Leone and the international community.

Events Leading to Lomé

In one of the arguments advanced on the causes of the conflict in Sierra Leone, Paul Richards (1996, 2005) argues that the rebellion was a result of the alienation of intellectuals influenced by Muammar Gaddafi's *Green Book*, coupled with the inability of rural youth to acquire farm land. Abdullah (1998) and, later, Rashid (2000) argue that the Revolutionary United Front (RUF) rebellion was a consequence of urban youth culture, alienation, and university student radicalism. Notwithstanding the polemics surrounding the causes and origin of the war, scholars agree that the RUF (rebellion) became monstrously destructive and consumed by resplendent banditry.

In 1991, armed members of the RUF rebel outfit attacked the village of Bomaru in eastern Sierra Leone. What was reported by government agencies as armed robbery turned out to be the beginning of a brutal insurgency that lasted for ten years and claimed over fifty thousand lives, with millions of people incapacitated and displaced (See Zack-Williams, Chapter 1 in this volume). Under the leadership of Foday Sankoh, the RUF declared its intention to overthrow the corrupt All Peoples' Congress (APC) government, led by President Joseph Saidu Momoh. The swift military successes of the RUF in capturing towns and villages exposed the vulnerabilities of the defense mechanism put in place by a weak state controlled by an incompetent and corrupt government.

In April 1992, thirteen months after the start of the RUF rebellion, a group of junior officers of the Sierra Leone Army, led by Captain Valentine Strasser, overthrew the APC government and established the National Provisional Ruling Council (NPRC). The overthrow of the APC government did not stop the war, as the RUF continued to capture territories, including the diamond-rich Kono district in Sierra Leone. The intensification of the war after the *coup d'etat* made it clear that, like the previous APC government, the NPRC was incapable of bringing the war to an end through military means. In 1996, the NPRC ousted Valentine Strasser in a palace coup, led by Brigadier Maada Bio, on the grounds that Strasser was bent on thwarting the democratic process. Though the RUF threatened to disrupt the 1996 elections, the elections went ahead as planned. The Sierra Leone People's Party won the elections, replacing the NPRC junta with a democratic civilian government. Before the election, the NPRC junta dismissed the threats of violence from the RUF. This dismissal of the RUF's relevance to the democratic process was a demonstration of arrogance and a gross underestimation of their potential to wreck untold havoc on the country. In spite of its opposition to the elections and its outcome, the RUF negotiated and signed the Abidjan Peace Accord with the newly elected Sierra Leone People's Party (SLPP) government, led by Ahmed Tejan-Kabbah, in November 1996.

The Abidjan Peace Accord

The Abidjan Peace Accord, signed between the government of Sierra Leone and the RUF, held the promise of peace. The agreement, among other things, made the following provisions: creation of a commission for the consolidation of peace; blanket amnesty for members of the RUF; RUF access to all political processes and its transformation into a political party; setting up of a committee to effect encampment, disarmament, demobilization, and resettlement; a downsized and restructured military and encampment; and subsequent repatriation of Executive Outcomes (EO) and other foreign troops. The RUF's acceptance of the terms of the Abidjan Peace Accord betrayed their weakness and battle weariness. The deployment of better trained mercenaries with superior military power such as the Executive Outcomes (EO) of South Africa may have been a catalyst in the RUF's willingness to sign the agreement. The RUF seemed to have been more concerned with seeking amnesty for their members and getting EO out of Sierra Leone than insisting on seeking government positions. These dynamics were to change considerably in 1999.

Neither party had any intention to adhere to the Abidjan Peace Accord. Shortly after signing the agreement, a splinter RUF group accused Foday Sankoh of trying to scuttle the peace agreement, and they dissociated themselves from Sankoh and attempted to replace him as their leader. Sankoh was later arrested in Nigeria; the RUF blamed the government of Sierra Leone for his arrest. The implementation of the Abidjan agreement was not to be realized, as a group of disgruntled soldiers, led by Major Johnny Paul Koroma, violently overthrew the government of Ahmed Tejan Kabbah in May 1997.

After the coup, Koroma invited his former adversaries, the RUF, to join him in a governing coalition referred to as the Armed Forces Revolutionary Council (AFRC; see Bangura, this volume). The coalition met stiff resistance from Sierra Leoneans, particularly students and the international community. The resistance of the students was met with merciless brutality from the junta-RUF coalition that resulted in the deaths of many students. To quell vociferous opposition to their regime, the junta signed a six-month peace plan on October 23, 1997, in Conakry, Guinea. The parties agreed to the following terms: cessation of hostilities; disarmament and demobilization; return of refugees; unconditional immunities from prosecution; and the restoration of constitutional governance within six months.

The Conakry Agreement

The Conakry Peace Plan was unlike other agreements in that the junta did not sign it with the government in exile; rather, they signed the pact with a five-man committee on Sierra Leone, set up by the Economic Community of West African States (ECOWAS), represented by the Nigerian foreign minister and his Guinean counterpart. Representatives of the Organization of African Unity (OAU) and the United Nations (UN) witnessed the ceremony. Unlike the Abidjan agreement, all parties agreed that the government of Tejan-Kabbah should be reinstated within six months. In addition, the reinstated government should form an "all-inclusive" government comprised of members of the exiled administration and RUF representatives. However, the peace agreement ended before the stipulated six months when the Economic Community of West African States Monitoring Group (ECOMOG), which was supposed to supervise the peace plan, expelled the junta regime and its forces from Freetown.

The forceful ejection, and the subsequent mob killings, of perceived supporters of the military junta in 1998 exacerbated the acrimony between the soldiers, on the one hand, and the government and civilians, on the other. After the restoration of President Kabbah, his government disbanded the military and prosecuted the coup plotters. Twenty-four soldiers were subsequently executed a week after they had been found guilty in a court martial that Amnesty International (AI) referred to as unfair (Amnesty International 1998). The executions, coupled with the disbandment of the army, were costly mistakes, as they threw a wrench in efforts at reconciliation and created another faction in the war comprised of renegade soldiers.

With the army disbanded, the already-weak central government relied heavily on a Nigerian-dominated ECOMOG and the Civil Defense Forces (CDF) for its security. Clearly, the new defense status assumed by ECOMOG altered its role from peacekeepers to protagonists, particularly from the RUF point of view. As Bangura and Zack-Williams discuss in this volume, ECOMOG was unable to defend the capital city when the combined forces of RUF and AFRC junta invaded and captured parts of the capital city, Freetown, on January 6, 1999. The ferocity and brutality of the attack forced the conflicting parties and the international community to realize that the war could not be won on the battlefields. Internal and external pressure forced the warring factions to agree to a peace summit in Lomé (Alao and Ero 2001; Francis 2000; and this volume, Shepler, Chapter 4; Conteh-Morgan, Chapter 8).

The Lomé Peace Accord

The Lomé Peace Accord, signed by the RUF and the government of Sierra Leone on July 7, 1999, was supposed to have marked the official end to the conflict. The accord brought about significant changes in the dynamics of the war. Part one of the agreement provided for the creation of a Cease-fire Monitoring Committee and a Joint Monitoring Commission, chaired by the United Nations Mission in Sierra Leone (UNAMSIL), with representatives from the RUF, CDF, and ECOMOG. The creation of UNAMSIL, and its subsequent chairing of the monitoring commissions, effectively ended ECOMOG's role as a *de jure* peacekeeping force in Sierra Leone. The removal of ECOMOG as a peacekeeping force may be connected with the human rights violations it was accused of committing (see Bangura, Chapter 2 in this volume).

Part two of the Lomé Peace Accord deals with governance issues, providing that: the RUF would be transformed into a political party; the members of the RUF would be allowed to hold public office; the RUF would be given cabinet appointments in a government of national unity; a commission for the consolidation of peace would be created; a commission for the management of strategic resources, national reconstruction, and development (CMRRD) would be created; and a council of elders would be developed. Part three of the agreement guarantees blanket amnesty for all combatants and collaborators; provides for a review of the constitution and appointment of a national electoral commission, with a mandate to organize new elections. The accord also called for the establishment of the Truth and Reconciliation Commission. The power-sharing provision of the accord allowed Foday Sankoh to become the chairman of CMRRD, with the rank of vice president, answerable only to the president. The RUF was offered four cabinet positions in the government. These concessions were heavily criticized by members of the public. In fact, civil society organizations demurred at these concessions on grounds that the concessions rewarded brutality.

Francis (2000, 366) criticizes the Lomé accord on moral grounds when he argues that the accord was no more than a barter of "crimes against humanity for peace and stability." Abraham (2001) also criticizes the accord on procedural grounds. He argues that the power-sharing provision was inappropriate because the accord allowed the RUF to "participate in a democratic political process through undemocratic means" since elections had already been conducted. While Francis's moral argument may be valid, it is important to understand the context in which those concessions were made. Clearly, the military option proved untenable, as the government of Sierra Leone was unable to protect its citizens from incessant rebel attacks, especially in the countryside. It is therefore understandable why the government chose peace and stability over continued war, as explicated by the former attorney general and, later, vice president, Solomon Berewa. In addition, we consider Abraham's criticism of the accord on procedural grounds as unfair. Free and fair elections do not preclude a government from negotiating power-sharing arrangements with a rebel group. The election of Ahmed Tejan Kabbah gave him the mandate to negotiate peace and give concessions to the RUF where necessary. It should be noted that the president had the constitutional power to appoint anyone to the cabinet as long as that individual was eligible to hold public office. As a result, the recognition of Foday Sankoh as answerable to only the president was not undemocratic. It did not, in our view, translate into creating another *de jure* vice president who could act in the absence of the president. It is our contention that the title was more or less ceremonial.

The Lomé accord marked significant departures from the previous two peace agreements; that is, in contrast to previous accords, the RUF made significant gains during the peace negotiations in Lomé: it effectively became part of the government and was charged with managing the country's mineral resources. The concessions given to the RUF in the Lomé accord contradict Abraham's (2001, 2003) argument that the rebel outfit negotiated from a position of weakness. Compared with the Abidjan Peace Accord, the RUF made forceful demands by asking for positions in the government during the Lomé negotiations. In the Abidjan Peace Accord, the RUF seemed to have been content with the cessation of hostilities, as their bases had been destroyed by government and mercenary forces. Rebel groups usually make unreasonable demands at peace negotiations, particularly when they negotiate from a position of strength. In Liberia, for example, Charles Taylor's National Patriotic Front of Liberia (NPFL) refused to accept a government of national unity with Samuel Doe (Adebajo 2002). Taylor had no intention of negotiating a war he thought he was going to win, noting, "The only good Doe is a dead Doe" (*Time* 2006). Analogously, in Zaire, now the Democratic Republic of Congo, Joseph Kabila, during peace talks with Mobutu Sese Seko, demanded the latter to resign as president. He threatened to advance to the capital Kinshasa if Mobutu ignored his demand (*Milwaukee Journal Sentinel* 1997). While the RUF-AFRC coalition was not as strong as Taylor's NPFL or Kabila's Alliance of Democratic Forces for the Liberation of Congo-Zaire (ADFLC), it was definitely not weak when juxtaposed with the government of Sierra Leone, which relied on ECOMOG for its national security. In fact, in the lead up to Lomé, it became evident that Nigeria was no longer willing to keep her troops in Sierra Leone. Thus, it is reasonable to argue that the government of Sierra Leone, rather than the RUF, negotiated the Lomé Peace Accord from a position of weakness.

With the signing of the accord, Foday Sankoh was released from prison and later took up residence in Freetown; United Nations peacekeepers were deployed; the CMRRD was created; cabinet positions were given to members of the RUF; and the disarmament, demobilization, and reintegration of ex-combatants were set to start. Notwithstanding these concessionary gestures made to the RUF, Sankohs's actions raised red flags about his sincerity and commitment to the peace accord (Francis 2000; Abraham 2001, 2003; Reno 2000). The RUF disarmed, imprisoned, and killed some UN peacekeepers. Sankoh also demonstrated inconsistency and disingenuousness by giving conflicting instructions to his fighters about the disarmament process. During this period, the RUF mobilized its fighters and advanced toward the capital city. The British intervened and prevented the capture of the capital in the name of protecting Western nationals. In response to the RUF's abjuration of the peace agreement, protesters headed to the residence of the rebel leader to register their disappointment. His body-guards fired into the crowd of innocent and unarmed civilians, killing a few people. Sankoh himself escaped the wrath of the protesters but was later arrested and detained. He died in prison shortly after the start of his trial for war crimes. President Kabbah relieved RUF members in the cabi-net of their duties, an action that practically rendered CMRRD defunct.

Many scholars cite the events highlighted above to describe the Lomé Peace Accord as a failure (Abraham 2001, 2003; Francis 2000; Reno 2000; Alao and Ero 2001; Adebajo 2002). While the government of Sierra Leone abnegated aspects of the accord after Foday Sankoh's incarceration, we argue that as imperfect as the Lomé Peace Accord and its implementation may have been (in this volume, see Tynes and Speed, Chapter 3; Shepler, Chapter 4; Henry, Chapter 5, and Conteh-Morgan, Chapter 8), it neither collapsed in its entirety nor failed in the larger scheme of things. The Lomé Peace Accord is largely responsible for the relative peace that postwar Sierra Leone is now experiencing. Democratic institutions such as the Truth and Reconciliation Commission and the National Election Commission are creatures of the accord. In addition, the Disarmament, Demobilization and Rehabilitation (DDR) program, coupled with the resettlement and rehabilitation programs, proved relatively successful. In fact, after the cap-ture of Sankoh in 2000, the cease-fire initiated by the signing of the Lomé accord was successfully maintained. Although President Kabbah dismissed RUF members from the cabinet, he maintained a largely inclusive admin-istration reflective of Sierra Leone's ethnic diversity.

Peace agreements are usually works in progress, wherein adjustments are made as the situation warrants. It is in this regard that the Lomé Peace Accord can be seen as a relative success. In order to reinforce the Lomé Peace Accord, some adjustments were made to the accord in Abuja, referred to as the Abuja cease-fire signed between the RUF and the govern-ment of Sierra Leone on November 10, 2000. The Abuja agreement shows renewed commitment to the Lomé Peace Accord, with the aim of creating a "conducive environment for fresh application of the Lomé Peace Accord" (The Government of Sierra Leone 2000). In spite of the successes noted above, the implementation of the Lomé accord is fraught with numerous challenges, as highlighted in the various chapters in this book. In addition to highlighting these challenges, the authors offer policy recommendations to overcome these challenges.

Structure of the Book

This volume is the first to critically analyze a peace accord that has played a key role in stabilizing one of the oldest states in West Africa. It is divided into two major parts: "Destination Lomé" and "Beyond Lomé." Part 1, "Destination Lomé," discusses events leading to the signing of the Lomé Peace Accord and the specificities of the articles contained therein. Part 2 analyzes postwar challenges in maintaining peace. The essays in this part highlight the numerous challenges facing postwar Sierra Leone. They show that there are hopeful signs that the peace so far attained can be sustained if the government focuses on policies that will lead to economic development, eliminate corruption, and provide employment opportunities.

Part 1: Destination Lomé

In Chapter 1, Zack-Williams traces the history of the civil war in Sierra Leone and the Lomé Peace Accord, signed between the government of Sierra Leone and the RUF rebels. Though he highlights the weaknesses of the accord, such as the gracious concessions made to the RUF and its leadership, he notes that the signing of the accord has, so far, entrenched peace leading to the holding of two successful democratic elections. Zack-Williams also highlights the vibrancy of the press and the independence of civil-society groups in postwar Sierra Leone.

In Chapter 2, Joseph J. Bangura explores the role of ECOMOG in the Sierra Leone conflict between 1997 and 2000. He argues that though the international community played a significant role in the peace process, ECOMOG helped establish a propitious atmosphere that resulted in the signing of the Lomé Peace Accord in 1999. Bangura also argues that the involvement of ECOMOG in daily combat operations, as it tried to protect the government of Sierra Leone, exposed it to accusation of being a protagonist force rather than peacekeepers. In addition, in demonstrating its loyalty to the government, the force engaged in blatant human rights abuses that undermined its credibility as a neutral intervenor or disinterested peacekeeper. Bangura concludes that ECOMOG should be maintained and transformed into a standby force, with the mandate to intervene and prevent the collapse of any ECOWAS-member state triggered by civil war or ravenous insurgents.

The chapter by Robert Tynes and Clark Speed examines the impact of Article 30 of the Lomé Peace Accord on child soldiers-combatants. They argue that in spite of the good intentions of the accord, the "concepts of re-integration and demobilization have mostly served the international community—foreign governments, the United Nations, as well as numerous NGOs—not necessarily the child soldiers themselves." Tynes and Speed believe that the accord should have focused heavily on the practical means of rehabilitation for child soldiers and less on the process by which this method was to be achieved, which merely benefited the executors of the plan. However, despite its shortcomings, the Lomé Peace Accord was the first to address the problem of child combatants. The authors note that the deficiencies inherent in the accord should be heeded so that future remedies for child soldiers will actually improve the lives of children immersed in conflicts.

Susan Shepler's chapter also analyzes the Lomé Peace Accord in relation to the protection of children. Like Tynes and Speed, Shepler argues that the Lomé Peace Accord was the first peace agreement to specifically mention the protection and integration of child soldiers in civil society. However, unlike Tynes and Speed, Shepler argues that protection of children, including child soldiers sanctioned by the Lomé Peace Accord, was influenced by the international climate at the time of the signing of the accord. She notes that while there were organizations such as Children Affected by War (CAW)—led by an indigene, Reverend Father Momoh—which protected the interests of children, the larger interests of children were protected by UNICEF and other international actors. Shepler further argues that while the Lomé accord made salient provisions for the protection of children and youths in general, the Sierra Leone government seemed to have reacted to "internationally defined concerns" rather than focusing on creating a conducive space for the development and caring of children and youths.

Part 2: Beyond Lomé

In this part, M. Douglas Henry, Fredline M'Cormack-Hale, Victor Davies, Earl Conteh-Morgan, and Marda Mustapha evaluate postwar economic developments and challenges in Sierra Leone. They recommend solutions to enable the government of Sierra Leone address its governance challenges.

In Chapter 5, Douglas Henry's examination of Article 27 of the Lomé accord, and its effect on citizens, refugees, and relief processes along the Sierra Leone-Guinea border, is informative. He argues that the Lomé Peace Accord allowed massive networks of relief agencies to access areas hitherto disregarded by the state. The presence of international Non Governmental Organizations (NGOs) in these marginalized communities brought to the fore the ambiguities of identities and national consciousness; that is, terms like "refugees" and "citizens" became negotiated entities in complicated and ambiguous ways. The discourse employed by relief agents along the

Sierra Leone-Guinea border resulted in the manipulation of identities by Sierra Leoneans and Guineans alike. The specificity emphasized by Article 27 of the Lomé accord on qualification for relief aid led to manipulation of the system. The action of Sierra Leoneans and Guineans occupying the once-marginalized border areas illustrates how identity along the margins of the state can resist "external definition, whether imposed upon it by the state or by state-like agents." Given the benefits of belonging to various categories, "the people at the margins" learned to undermine attempts at bifurcation by flocking in and out of the established categories. In sum, Article 27 of the Lomé accord exposed the fluidity of identity categories as "refugees could become citizens; citizens could become refugees."

Chapter 6, by Fredline M'Cormack-Hale, probes the intersection between NGO assistance and democratization in postwar Sierra Leone. Using a variety of research tools and statistical analyses, M'Cormack-Hale argues that exposure to NGO projects results in strengthened democracy, when measured at the level of attitudes, beliefs and behavioral patterns. M'Cormack-Hale shows that participation in NGO projects affects attitudes, beliefs, and political behavior to some degree; that is, NGO affiliates show a higher degree of political and civic engagement. Because of their increased political knowledge, this group of respondents is more critical of the practice of democracy in postwar Sierra Leone than their counterparts with no NGO affiliation.

In sum, M'Cormack-Hale maintains that there is no "clear answer to the impact of NGOs on democracy strengthening [in postwar Sierra Leone]." In addition, the research findings show that NGO activities increased political consciousness among a group of participants. She concludes that given the range and breadth of their activities in a nascent state reeling from a devastating civil war, like Sierra Leone, NGOs contribute to undermining state-society relations, possible insecurity, and alienation of some citizens. She also notes that the policies of decentralization can be problematic and need to be addressed. If democracy is to be strengthened in postwar Sierra Leone, the government must embark on good governance, encourage true democratic practice, and empower citizens with increased political knowledge.

In Chapter 7, Victor Davies evaluates Sierra Leone's economic challenges in the post-Lomé and postwar era. He argues that the overarching economic challenge of Sierra Leone over the years has been to manage its rich natural resources for the benefit of all citizens. Although Sierra Leone is considered to be one of the richest countries in terms of natural and mineral resources in Africa, a majority of its population lives below the poverty line. The civil war and its aftermath have exacerbated this situation. To consolidate the peace gained so far, and in order to raise living standards, Davies argues that pro-growth and employment creation policies, particularly for the large number of unemployed youths, should be adopted. He asserts that with an efficient management mechanism, Sierra Leone would be in a strong position to negotiate favorable terms with investment firms, curtail corruption, and enhance government's capacity to control its resources better. Davies believes widespread corruption and general inefficiencies underline the need to separate the functions of policy management, spending, and retail service delivery. He recommends privatization in retail service delivery of health and education services to promote competition and efficiency.

Earl Conteh-Morgan notes that for peacebuilding to be perdurable, the social and political environment that fosters intolerable inequality, historical grievances, and adversarial interactions must be transformed. This means dismantling structures that contribute to violent conflict. Conteh-Morgan argues that to a large extent, the Lomé Peace Accord is an "externally driven treaty whose objective was to ensure the sovereignty of the Sierra Leonean state," with little or no emphasis on abating the insecurities of individuals and groups. In other words, the Lomé accord and the peacebuilding process underlines procedural aspects of peacebuilding, such as peacekeeping, which involves monitoring cease-fire violations, demobilization and rehabilitation of combatants, and humanitarian relief by the international community. Conteh-Morgan further argues that the benefits of these initiatives are short term, and merely ensure the integrity of the state rather than ensuring a sustainable or long-term peace. In postwar Sierra Leone, sustainable peace means strengthening and reasserting normative structures that enable and empower individuals and groups to share common identities, understandings, and expectations that would enhance and entrench social order for the benefit of the masses critical in maintaining state security. Conteh-Morgan assertively notes that state-centric or externally imposed peacebuilding measures do not strongly encourage postwar societies such as Sierra Leone to critically reflect on internal dynamics that can produce positive peace and a perennially secured environment.

Like Mustapha and Davies argue in this volume, Conteh-Morgan believes that for postwar Sierra Leone to achieve sustainable positive peace, employment opportunities for youths and others must be created, health care insurance must be guaranteed for all—especially the traumatic segment of the population—criminal activities must be curbed, and food security should be provided for the masses. This also means international assistance must effectively target the vulnerable segments of the population.

In Chapter 9, Marda Mustapha argues that while the Lomé Peace Accord secured negative peace, Sierra Leone is still grappling with the persistence of structural violence. Mustapha contends that the prevalence of structural violence in postwar nations like Sierra Leone can be attributed to global inequalities stimulated by the formulation and implementation of neoliberal global economic policies. These policies are channeled through international financial institutions such as the World Bank and the International Monetary Fund. It is clear that while many of the policies formulated and implemented by the international financial institutions benefit the donors, it is difficult for countries like Sierra Leone to effectively deal with their internal structural violence and resultant inequalities. Therefore, solutions for the structural problems facing postwar Sierra Leone would have to include, but are not limited to, analyzing and implementing solutions at the global and national levels. Mustapha recommends that Sierra Leone, as a postwar nation, should revisit its priorities if structural violence and inequalities are to be effectively curtailed or minimized.

Summing up, the Lomé Peace Accord indeed achieved a number of firsts, as elucidated by the chapters included in this volume. Like Dick Simpson points out in the Afterword, Sierra Leone has achieved negative peace, even if "existential insecurity" still exists. The war trials concluded in the conviction of leaders of the RUF, AFRC, and members of the government-sponsored civil militia, the Kamajors. Charles Taylor, former leader of the National Patriotic Front of Liberia, and later head of state of Liberia, stands accused of supporting the RUF, and he is currently on trial at the UN-backed court at The Hague. The lead prosecutor for the Special Court of Sierra Leone points out that the trials resulted in the first convictions "for using child soldiers, the first convictions in world history for a 'campaign of terror,' the first convictions for sexual slavery and the first convictions for 'bush wives,' that is women who were conscripted into forced marriages." In addition, new national and local governments have been established with the successful holding of local council elections since the signing of the Lomé Peace Accord. In spite of these positive developments, Simpson notes that the integration of all combatants has not been successful. Economic disparities continue to exist, accompanied by illiteracy and poverty, especially among the youth, and public corruption continues to drain the resources of the country. He observes that despite all these challenges, Sierra Leoneans believe in a bright future for the country as a whole.

References

Abdullah, Ibrahim. 1998. Bush path to destruction: Origin and character of the Revolutionary United Front/Sierra Leone. *Journal of Modern African Studies* 36: 203–35.

Abraham, Arthur. 2001. Dancing with the chameleon: Sierra Leone and the elusive quest for peace. *Journal of Contemporary African Studies* 19 (2): 205–28.

———. 2003. The elusive quest for peace: From Abidjan to Lomé. In *Between democracy and terror: The Sierra Leone civil war*, ed. I. Abdullah. Dakar, Senegal: Council for the Development of Social Science Research in Africa.

Adebajo, Adekeye. 2002. *Building peace in West Africa: Liberia, Sierra Leone and Guinea-Bissau*. Boulder, CO: Lynne Rienner.

Alao, Abiodun, and Comfort Ero. 2001. Cut short for taking short cuts: The Lomé peace agreement on Sierra Leone. *Civil Wars* 4 (3): 117–34.

Amnesty International. 1998. Execution of 24 soldiers after an unfair trial: A blow to reconciliation in Sierra Leone. *News Service*, Amnesty International Index: AFR 51/20/98

Bangura, Yusuf. 2000. Strategic policy failure and governance in Sierra Leone. *Journal of Modern African Studies* 38 (4): 551–77.

Francis, David. 2000. Torturous path to peace: The Lomé accord and postwar peacebuilding in Sierra Leone. *Security Dialogue* 31 (3): 357–73.

Milwaukee Journal Sentinel. 1997. Zaire's Mobutu, rebel leader to meet for peace talks: Kabila expects president to hand power during summit. April 30.

Rashid, Ishmail. 2000. Student radicals, lumpen youth and the origins of revolutionary groups in Sierra Leone 1977–1996. In *Between democracy and terror*, ed. I. Abdullah. Dakar, Senegal: Council for the Development of Social Science Research in Africa.

Reno, William. 2000. No Peace for Sierra Leone. *Review of African Political Economy* 84:325–48.

Richards, Paul. 1996. *Fighting for the rain forest: War youth and resources in Sierra Leone*. Portsmouth: Heinemann.

———. 2005. To fight or to farm? Agrarian dimensions of the Mano River conflicts (Sierra Leone and Liberia). *African Affairs* 104 (417): 571–90.

The Government of Sierra Leone. 2000. Abuja cease-fire fire agreement. *The Sierra Leone Web*, November. http://www.sierra-leone.org/ceasefire1100.html.

Time. 2006. Liberia in the heart of darkness. March 29. http://www.time.com/time/magazine/article/0,9171,971095,00.html.

Part I

Destination Lomé

1

Sierra Leone beyond Lomé

Challenges and Failures

Tunde Zack-Williams

Introduction

In March 1991, war broke out in the southeastern corner of Sierra Leone, close to the Liberian border, when a group of fighters consisting of exiled Sierra Leoneans, Liberians, and Burkinabes entered the country from Liberia, with the avowed aim of overthrowing the All Peoples' Congress (APC) government that had ruled the country since 1968. For a long time, the conflict was confined to the south and southeastern provinces, far removed from Freetown, the capital, where the rebel leader was seen by the ruling elites as a mysterious character, and whom few people in the capital seemed to have heard about. However, in May 1997, the rebels were able to enter the capital, thanks to a military revolt by the country's armed forces—under the leadership of a young major, Johnny Paul Koroma—which overthrew the newly elected president, Ahmed Tejan Kabba. The junta, calling itself the Armed Forces Revolutionary Council (AFRC), then went on to invite Foday Sankoh, the leader of the rebel movement known as the Revolutionary United Front (RUF) to form a people's army. The coup, and the rebel's entry into the capital, resulted in widespread violence and destruction. During this time, the local prison was emptied of all violent convicts, who in turn unleashed untold suffering upon the civilian population before they were ejected from the capital by the Nigerian-led Economic Community of West African States Monitoring Group (ECOMOG) forces the following year.

The ragtag army of the RUF (Abdullah and Muana 1998) proved a good match for the ill-equipped, highly politicized, and undisciplined government forces, as they captured large areas of the country, including the diamond-rich eastern province containing the epicenters of diamond mining in Koidu Town, located in the Kono District; and Tongo Field in the Kenema District (Musah 2000). It soon became clear to the Sierra Leonean authorities that the RUF was a social movement of a different kind, the likes of which the country had not seen since independence in 1961. The war precipitated the end of the long rule of the one-party dictatorship of the All Peoples' Congress (APC) that had been in power since 1968, during which time the act of kleptocracy was perfected, laying the foundation for much of the grievances of the rebel groups. In March 1996, in the middle of the war, and following agitation from a section of civil society for a return to democratic governance, the junta decided to organize elections for a return to civilian rule, which the country's oldest political party, the Sierra Leone People's Party, won both the parliamentary and presidential elections. The party was led by Mr. Ahmed Tejan Kabba, a former United Nations (UN) bureaucrat. As noted earlier, in May of the following year, the new civilian administration was removed from office by elements within the armed forces, led by Major Johnny Paul Koroma, who in turn were driven out of the capital by troops of the ECOMOG. A group of hard-core elements of the AFRC remained in the eastern section of the capital. Known as the West Side Boys, they continued to harass the civilian population in the capital and to engage in widespread banditry.

One important characteristic of the war was the widespread use of child soldiers by both sides: the rebel RUF and its ally the AFRC, on the one hand, and government forces and their allies the Civil Defense Forces—including the *Kamajors, Donsos, Tamaboro, Gbethis*, and *Kapras*—on the other. Whilst many of these young fighters were conscripted into the fighting forces, many joined voluntarily (Peters and Richards 1998), largely as a result of rupture in the intergenerational bargain through which, in less troubled times, one generation provides a nurturing environment for the next (Zack-Williams 2001a). Another feature of the war is that much of the violence was directed at the civilian population, impelling one commentator to identify a link between emergency institutions and increasing violence on civilian populations (Hoffman 2004), which is discussed further in the section named "Explicating the Civil War in Sierra Leone," The break down in the command structure of the army and the recruitment of army personnel from among déclassé elements in the urban areas saw the growth of army personnel, who were prepared to work with the rebels, as well as looting the property of civilians. These soldier-rebels were promptly referred to as *sobel* (Abdullah and Muana 1998; Zack-Williams 1999). Keen in his book, *Conflict and collusion in Sierra Leone*, referred to this as: "sell game: a strangely co-operative conflict" (Keen 2005, 107). There were a number of agreements and accords signed by both sides, which were not fully implemented or observed, including aspects of the Lomé Peace Accord, which rebel leader Foday Sankoh signed in July 1999, but immediately proceeded to violate as the last Nigerian ECOMOG troops left in May 2000, when he seized the opportunity to launch a putsch for total state power.

The focus of this chapter consists of an analysis of both the Lomé accord and the policies of the civilian governments of President Ahmed Tejan Kabba, arguing that both failed to address the fundamental causal problems of the war. However, before addressing these important questions, it is imperative to look at how a once peaceful people were gradually transformed or pushed into becoming perpetrators of violence on each other.

From a Land of Cowardice to a Land of Extreme Brutality

Sierra Leone's longest-serving ruler and founder of the APC, Mr. Siaka Probyn Stevens, is widely reported to have averred that his people were cowards who could bark but not bite. In other words, the security network, which he had built up in his almost twenty years' rule, was so effective that it would nip any potential uprising in the bud. To help him achieve this, he skillfully established himself as a "modern-day Bonaparte" and as tracing his origin to the major ethnic groups and major regions in the country (the north, the western area, and the south). Through his early job as a mineworker union organizer, he emphasized his identity with workers; as father of the nation; as fountain of honor; and as serving the interests of all classes (Zack-Williams 1985).

In his quest for a one-party state, Stevens silenced all opposition with a series of allegations, trials, and executions for plotting and attempted coups involving both civilians and the military. In one such case, a corporal in the army, Foday Sankoh, was accused of plotting to overthrow the APC, and was tried and subsequently dismissed from the army, only to return years later as leader of the rebel Revolutionary United Front, this time, seeking revenge. Far from mobilizing his people for the task of national development, Stevens depoliticized his people and they became dependent on his loyal chiefs for local governance. In 1972, district and urban councils were abolished and replaced by nominated members appointed by his government (Farnthorpe 2001). This policy had a devastating effect on the caliber of those who were unleashed to the political center, since there were no institutions, such as local governments, in which they could learn or practice the act of local governance. This and other policies forced many technocrats and professionals to vote with their feet as they sought pastures green, further depleting the pool from which cadres could be recruited.

The period after 1972, which saw the end of the brief period of "coalition" government, marked the consolidation of the patrimonial state through patron-client relationships and a constellation of dependence networks, running from the rural unemployed to politicians at the center, via local "big men," local chiefs, and powerful traders. This whole mechanism, which has been referred to as the "shadow state" (Reno 1995), like all patrimonial states needed resources to ensure smooth running of the clientelistic networks. However, this flow of resources was scampered by economic mismanagement and corruption, on the one hand, and the import-led inflation and consequences of the structural adjustment programs (Mohan and others 2000), on the other. The alluvial deposits of diamonds provided a major source of resources for supporting the patrimonial network. In 1970, Stevens nationalized the former British-owned Sierra Leone Selection Trust (SLST), which was now called the National Diamond Mining Company (NDMC) Limited. Within a decade, the structure and operations of the company had been informalized as Stevens and his cronies in the party, including Paramount Chiefs in the diamond districts, hived off large tracks of the company's land and operations to private ownership (Zack-Williams 1995b).

Politically, Stevens's rule was also remarkable for the introduction of thuggery in the body politic of the nation, as young men in particular were organized as political thugs to harass and torment opposition politicians; some of these same young people would soon be transformed into cadres for the RUF rebellion. After almost twenty-five years in power, the ruling APC had transformed the Weberian formulation of a rational legal bureaucracy into a charismatic form, marked by "authoritarian centralism," and the gradual disenfranchisement of the entire population, as "democratic elections" were transformed into "elections by unopposed and elections by announcement."[1]

As noted earlier, charismatic or patrimonial forms of governance are premised on the ability of the patriarch replenishing his patrimonial network or shadow state. By the early 1980s, following the excesses of the Organization of African Unity (OAU) meeting in Sierra Leone in 1980, the mounting debt accumulated through corruption and economic mismanagement, as well as the falling value and volume of the country's exports, all helped to push both the economy and society to a crisis point (Zack-Williams 1990). Mindful of the rising tide of resentment, Stevens decided to hand over power to his much-trusted force commander and kinsman, Brigadier Joseph Saidu Momoh. This was a bitter snub to his heir apparent and founding member of the APC, Sorie Ibrahim Koroma, who had deputized for Stevens on several occasions. Koroma was renowned for his no-nonsense attitude toward opponents, but was seen as more probing than his leader. Momoh's elevation to the high office of state created problems within the APC as well as the country at large. Without the political skills and support of his predecessor, Momoh faced challenges from within and outside the party. The result was that both party and country were plunged into a series of political and economic crises, the former resulting in the execution of Momoh's deputy, Francis Minah, who was accused of treason and of trying to exploit the unpopularity of the new president to organize a coup. The execution of Minah incensed many people and exacerbated ethnic and regional tensions in the country (Zack-Williams 2001b).

Explicating the Civil War in Sierra Leone

There are various explanations that have been advanced as causal factors for the war in Sierra Leone, and whilst some of them are interlinked, many are historically constituted (Farnthorpe 2001; Peters and Richards 1998; Richards 2005). This section will examine some of these factors by drawing attention to how they have impacted upon policy makers in general, and the Lomé Peace Accord and postwar developments in particular. In drawing attention to these factors, we will then be able to take stock of what has been achieved since Lomé. The initial point to note is that of the "revolutionary imperative" for change which existed prior to the emergence of Foday Sankoh and the RUF. What was needed was the spark that would ignite the revolutionary zeal of the Sierra Leonean people. Indeed, the arrival of the nonideological RUF and its nihilist tendencies deprived the Sierra Leonean people of the opportunity to make history by ejecting their oppressors and tormentors from state power. We have drawn attention to how counterdiscourses were treated by the APC in their quest for total domination and ensuring a quiescent population. Twenty-three years of APC political authoritarianism and economic mismanagement had sapped the energy of the Sierra Leonean people, as a once proud nation was brought to its knees by APC misrule. By the beginning of the 1990s, their capital was in total darkness, having been transformed into an electricity-free zone, save for the rumbling of private generators; hyperinflation had taken hold of the economy; public officials went for several months without salaries; and both agricultural and mineral output were smuggled out of the countries porous borders, thus depriving the state of vital foreign exchange. The engulfing economic crisis resulted in the long road to the international financial institutions (IFIs) and the implementation of

Structural Adjustment Programs (SAPs). The devastating shock effects of SAPs produced a massive deflationary effect on the economy, resulting in widespread unemployment, dilapidating infrastructure, and cost-recovery strategy, which hit the poorest of the poor, especially women and girls (Zack-Williams 1995a). Structural adjustment programs designed to rectify macroeconomic imbalances in payment further weakened the ability of the people to challenge their exploitative leaders, whilst those middle-class professionals and technocrats with marketable skills voted with their feet to escape the phenomenon of middle-class poverty.

One of the least helpful explanations of the war is that which is associated with Paul Collier, a World Bank economist who dismisses the grievances of the masses against imperialist and domestic exploitation, corruption, and totalitarianism; instead, he argues, "Conflicts are more likely to be caused by economic opportunities than by grievance" (Collier 2000, 91).[2] In his view, the economic agenda outweighs any grievance that oppressed people in Africa could invoke, and, as such, policy toward conflict must reflect this reality. In the world of Collier, "The objective factors that might contribute to grievance, such as income and asset inequality, ethnic and religious divisions and political repression, do not increase the risks of conflict" (Collier 2000, 110).

In this grand narrative, designed to explicate conflicts in Africa through quantitative indices, Collier has tried to impose a systematic, empiricist view of a phenomenon that requires qualitative and historical analyses. The raison d'être of this type of approach is to impose mathematical and statistical methods in analyzing social phenomena—to affect predictability—in order to celebrate "science." However, as David Willer and Judith Willer warned over three decades ago, this type of scientism is nothing more than pseudoscience (Willer and Willer 1973). For example, in the historical analysis of the rise of the RUF by Ibrahim Abdullah, it is clear that the events that led to the rise of the RUF and its nihilist leader had nothing to do with predatory desires for the country's raw material, but a misguided belief that he (Foday Sankoh) could lead "revolutionaries" trained in Libya and Ghana to change *de system* (Abdullah 1997). As Gberie has pointed out, in the case of Sierra Leone, the exchange of diamonds for weapons did not figure in the RUF war against a corrupt and bankrupt APC government until much later in the war (Gberie 2005). This type of analysis tends to trivialize the struggle of the African masses for change and for liberation from economic and political oppression. As a post-cold-war conflict, it was not possible to have superpower sponsors, as was the case with the wars of liberation in the 1960s and 1970s; though in the case of Sierra Leone, Colonel Gaddafi was initially a major sponsor of Charles Taylor and Foday Sankoh (Abdullah 1997; Gberie 2005), two people who had vowed to aid each other's revolutionary effort well before the emergence of the phenomenon of "blood diamonds" in West Africa. Furthermore, could this economistic model help us predict the conflict in Kenya in early 2008? What natural resources were being coveted and offered to multinationals by Odinga and Kibaki? By the same token, by valorizing an economistic model at the expense of the struggle by ordinary Africans to demand a say on how they should be governed and by whom, this model depoliticizes the people's desire for progress and hijacks their struggles.

Paul Richards—in his book *Fighting for the Rain Forest* (1996) and in a number of articles (1995, 2005)—was one of the first authors to systematically analyze the conflict in Sierra Leone. The strength of his work is that it benefits from prolonged periods of ethnographic work in the region over the course of several decades (Richards 1985, 1986). In his first major analysis of the war, Richards challenged American writer Robert Kaplan's (1994) portrayal of the wars in Liberia and Sierra Leone as irrational and a result of culture clash, a position described by Richards as "Malthus-with-guns" or the "New Barbarism." For Kaplan, the post-cold-war conflicts in the third world, and those in Liberia and Sierra Leone in particular, were the product of culture clash based on resource competition and environmental degradation, resulting in a rash of localized and uncontrollable armed conflicts, social banditry, and criminogenic apolitical actions. In short, armed conflicts in Africa, unlike those in the European theaters of war, are irrational and senseless. Kaplan's occidental contempt of social movements in Africa is complete when he observed, in a Clausewitzian fashion, that whilst European wars should be seen as the continuation of diplomacy by any other means, by contrast, African conflicts (new wars) are not fully understood by the participants themselves, as the wars are products of environmental crises to which Africans were presumably hapless victims.

In the context of the "New Barbarism," it is argued that the roots of African conflicts can be traced to ethnic and religious conflicts, with the object of the war game not directed toward land appropriation and control of population but toward acquiring resources for co-modification—minerals like diamonds and coltan—as well as to obtain sylvan culture. In addition, Africa's new wars do not result in pitch battles between two standing armies; instead, the targets of violence are the civilians, in order to attract the attention, goodwill, and resources of the NGOs and international community.[3]

For Richards to attribute the conflicts in Sierra Leone to environmental factors, and to suggest that the young combatants he interviewed were irrational, is indicative of the lack of understanding of the reasons why the youth of Sierra Leone rose up against their perceived oppressors: the traditional rulers, injustice from adults, and the failing state that has deprived them of education and social citizenship. Thus, Richards observed, "Unable to perceive the practical rationality of war . . . New Barbarism assumes that the conflict makes no sense according to outsiders and must be throwback to some African 'Dark Age'" (Richards 1996, xxi).

Unlike the "greed not grievance" argument, Richards premised his analysis on the role of agrarian factors, rooted in domestic slavery. Most of his informants were from rural backgrounds who traced their grievances to agrarian issues; thus, he rejected "the urban gang model." Many of his informants drew attention to the abuses of the "tribal administrative court" system, which they experienced, as well as widespread rural poverty and injustice, with many being forced to work for the traditional rulers and elders with little time to work for themselves. He argued that for these descendants of slaves, the RUF slogan "no more master, no more slave" had a positive resonance, which will bring an end to claims of "woman damage" (young men often falsely accused of interfering with the wives of powerful men) and the right of elite men to demand community labor. According to Richards, the *coup de grace* was the impact of SAPs, which triggered the disappearance of state presence (institution and personnel) from the interior during the 1970 and 1980s, and the nonpayment of salaries to government workers in the 1980s. The gradual disappearance of the state from the rural areas strengthened the grip of the rural gerontocrats and traditional rulers. Unemployment rose among both the young uneducated and school-leavers, making them even more vulnerable and dependent on the predatory village elites. Many would like to see an end to compulsory bridewealth transactions, land insecurity, and unpaid labor. Unfortunately, both the main political parties—the SLPP and the APC—have embarked on a policy of indirect rule, which not only valorizes the traditional leaders, but also seeks to entrench their positions in the rural areas.

Richards's work has come under much criticism, mainly from Yusuf Bangura (1997b), Ibrahim Abdullah (1997), and Edward Sawyer (2008). Sawyer challenged Richards's assertion that the conflict was fuelled by the crisis within chiefdom authority and the tension between rural youth and elders. Citing Farnthorpe's (2001) call for institutional reform of chiefdoms, through greater transparency and re-bureaucratization to prevent corruption, Sawyer argued that chiefdom authority is far from waning and that chiefs are better placed than politicians to protect the poor and vulnerable. In a sample survey of all the districts in the country, he found that the vast majority of respondents (78 percent) agreed that they felt that traditional authorities, when compared to other conflict resolutions in conflict agencies, were superior. To argue that chiefs were superior to corrupt state officials in remote Freetown does not negate the negative role the anachronistic institution of chieftaincy has played in the country's politics. The vacillating role of the thirteen paramount chiefs in declaring for the party with the largest seat in the House of Representatives (as was the tradition) was a crucial factor leading to the first military intervention in the country (Cartwright 1970). Furthermore, the "popularity" of the chief's vis-à-vis the corrupt politicians at the center should not be read as a negation of the cry from young men and women, described as a "potential social time bomb" ready to explode at any time.[4] Furthermore, tension with chiefdom authorities is a live issue for postwar district councils.

One systematic attempt to locate the origin of the war in rebellious youth culture is that of Ibrahim Abdullah (1997, 2004), who has questioned Richards initial argument about the role of excluded intellectuals, and "his heavy reliance on resources of the forest," at the expense of analyzing the "the central political importance of rebellious youth culture" (1997, 50). Both Abdullah and Richards tried to focus their research within class analysis: the latter, around rural class differentiation, and the former, utilizing urban class delineation. Abdullah argues that whilst the radical tradition of the Pan-Africanist I. T. A. Wallace-Johnson has dissipated from the center, it did not mean the "end of radical labour/political agitation" (1997, 46); this is evidenced in the urban slum area, a product of the petit bourgeois postcolonial mode of accumulation.

This radical youth counterculture emerged out of the traditional masquerades in the urban areas, such as the *odelays* (secret society masquerades). As cultural genre of the subaltern, it was despised by the elites, who denigrated it and put a Manichean divide between elite youth culture and what Abdullah called the "lumpen" or *rarray boys'* culture. However, the representation of the "lumpen culture" started to change in the 1970s with the arrival of curious middle-class youth (mainly school children) and "other respectable groups." The spatial location of the *potes* (*location for socialization of these young people*), with easy access to drinks, drug smoking, and prostitution, soon transformed this location into a recruiting ground for political thugs during the long reign of the APC. These thugs were used against opposition parties and any who dared challenge the party, including students. According to Abdullah, these new recruits to the *potes* soon became active participants, many dropping out of school to frequent the *potes* and to solidify their rebellious and nonconformity, making many contributions to the emerging popular culture. As the economy continued to decline in the 1970 and 1980s (an issue that does not figure much in Abdullah's analysis), many university students started patronizing the potes, providing the core of "organic intellectuals," (Abdullah 1997, 52) and these, according to Abdullah, were accorded higher status, no longer *rarray boys*, but now *savis man dem*, that is,

educated or well-informed men. These hybridized men brought political philosophy and ideology to discussions of the plight of the continent
through the eyes of Pan-Africanists such as Kwame Nkrumah, Marcus
Garvey, and I. T. A. Wallace-Johnson, and revolutionaries such as Frantz
Fanon, Fidel Castro, and Vladimir Lenin.

Abdullah went on to trace the dynamics of the potes, its members, and
the various influences on young people, including socialist ideas, Pan-Afri-
canism, and Mummar Gaddafi's *Green Book*. Soon at Fourah Bay College,
the country's premier higher-education institution, a radical student leadership emerged, not only to do battle with the college authorities, but also
to act vicariously for the working masses. The first test came in 1977 following the official visit of former Zambian leader Kenneth Kaunda, when
the college students decided to demonstrate in solidarity with the workers in Zambia. At this time, the country was under attack and pressure
from the racist regime of rebel leader Ian Smith in what was then Rho-
desia. The demonstration soon spread to the convocation ceremonies of
the university, where the chancellor, no other than President Stevens, was
jeered and heckled by students who were demanding his resignation and
new elections. Meanwhile, future RUF leader Foday Sankoh, who had been
dismissed from the army for his part in a coup plot, was also delving in radical student-cum-Pan-Africanist politics, and underwent military training
with other Sierra Leoneans in Libya and Ghana during the regime of Flight
Lieutenant Jerry Rawlings. According to Abdullah, Sankoh met Rawlings in
1988 in Freetown, and there was a subsequent agreement between the two
men to help each other in their respective struggles for national liberation
(Abdullah 1997).

The Nature of the War

By all accounts, the civil war in Sierra Leone was a very brutal one. The
figures of those demobilized ranged from forty-five to seventy thousand
armed fighters (Richards 2005), and some seventy-five thousand people lost
their lives (Sawyer 2008). Even larger numbers were injured, with at least
six hundred amputees who survived their ordeals (Lord 2000, 13). Almost
half the population was internally displaced, with thousands living as refugees in neighboring countries. According to Gbla (2003), 12 percent (i.e.,
five thousand) of the fighters were children; many were volunteers seeking
revenge for the destruction of their country and their education (Peters and
Richards 1998); and others were abducted from areas that had been overrun
by the rebels. Government forces, including the Republic of Sierra Leone
Armed Forces, recruited street children during the period of the NPRC junta

from 1992 through 1996, which ended twenty-four years of continuous APC rule. The Civil Defense Forces (CDF), allies of the government, also recruited children, and many were used in gathering intelligence from the enemy, as porters carrying weapons and ammunitions as well as lobbing grenades behind enemy lines and in crowds to create havoc. It was argued that in comparison with senior commanders, children had no familial responsibility and were therefore dispensable and ready for frontline duties (Zack-Williams 2006).

The utilization of children in war created major social problems, as they were impelled to unleash untold violence on the civilian population, including their communities and families, in order to helm them even more firmly into their fighting units. Many of them were victims of the war who were not only killed and injured, but who also formed part of a lost generation—many were orphaned and also lost out on education. These were some of the problems that the various accords had to address:

- Peace to a nation torn asunder by senseless and vicious war
- Demobilization of former combatants; reconciliation, in particular former child soldiers, with surviving family; and reintegration into society with skills or training
- Rehabilitation of collapsed infrastructure, including schools, hospitals, rural clinics, private and public buildings, mines, roads, bridges, and farms
- Rebuilding of political institutions, including the weak and collapsed state
- Sustainable peace in order to attract much-needed inward investments
- Installation of an accountable and democratic government that would ensure the country's resources were used judiciously.

In Search of Sustainable Peace

The first formal meeting of the two sides in the war resulted in the Abidjan Peace Accord, signed in November 1996 by the newly elected government of President Kabba and the RUF leader Foday Sankoh. From the beginning, Sankoh was less than enthusiastic about the agreement, as he refused to send representatives to the demobilization committee, which, as Bangura (1997a) has argued, undermined the work of the peace commission and the disarmament process as a whole. The accord called for an immediate cessation of all fighting, amnesty for all RUF fighters, and the transformation of the RUF into a political organization, as well as the establishment of a leader, a move that was questioned and contested by the "bush commanders," including Bockarie Masquita, Sankoh's loyal lieutenant.

The signing of the treaty was accompanied by renewed hostility between the RUF and the Kamajors and between the Kamajors and the Sierra Leone army. As part of the accord, the RUF was given blanket immunity from prosecution for war crimes and other atrocities perpetuated upon the civilian population, and a joint monitoring group was set up between the government and the RUF to police the cease-fire. The treaty envisaged a power-sharing regime; called for electoral, judicial and police reform, human rights observation, and probity in government; and called for the need to strengthen the integrity of the National Electoral Council in order to render it an effective force. The accord also set up a peace commission; unfortunately, no time frame was set for its deliberation and very little was said about the rights of women and retribution for rights abuse during the war (Gberie 2000). The accord was finally killed by the events of May 1997 and the January 1999 invasion of the capital.

The generosity obtained in Abidjan convinced the RUF leadership that the victory, which was not won on the battlefield, could be obtained at the negotiation table, as Sankoh rejected any suggestion that the UN peace-keeping troops (UNAMSIL) should be deployed in the country following the departure of Executive Outcomes (EO), which had been invited by the government to help push the RUF out of the diamond field in Kono. Sankoh also called for the removal of all foreign troops, meaning the Nigerian-led ECOMOG forces, which had prevented RUF regulars from overrunning the capital.

After the failure of the Abidjan accord, the next peace talk between the two warring parties was the Conakry Peace Plan of June 26, 1997, which set out a seven-point plan to return Sierra Leone to constitutional rule following the coup by the AFRC. This agreement also shared one important feature with both the Abidjan accord and, later, the Lomé accord: the blanket immunity from prosecution for all parties, which some writers see as the African paradigm of conflict resolution (Francis 2008).

Lomé Peace Accord, 1999

The Lomé peace talks came in the wake of the Abidjan and Conakry accords, as well as the dreadful attack on the capital in January 1999 by the RUF, in which scores of private dwellings and government buildings were destroyed, and thousands of innocent civilians killed or seriously wounded. President Kabba failed to utilize the weak strategic position of the RUF prior to 1999 to impose a settlement on the rebels; instead, by the beginning of 1999, the rebels had seized the initiative by occupying some two-thirds of the country, thus transforming the fortune of the government and its allies, ECOMOG and the civil defense forces. Indeed, the mayhem caused by the RUF in the January 1999 attack on the capital was an important factor impelling the international community to take the situation in Sierra Leone seriously, to urge the Sierra Leone government to sue for peace, and propelling "regional and international actors to impose half-baked solutions to a situation that requires the use of force and strict application of international law," as they were subsequently forced to do (Nzongola-Ntalaja 2000, 46).

According to Nzongola-Ntalaja (2000, 46), the Lomé agreements were predicated on the wrong supposition—that the rebels would take advantage of their strategic position in the field to end the war "in the process of national reconciliation and reconstruction." Despite the widespread allegation of human rights abuses, and the fact that the RUF and its ally, the AFRC, had removed a legitimately constituted regime from power, the RUF was given equal status at the negotiation table with the government they had removed from power.

This process of political incorporation and political immaturity on the part of the RUF soon became clear at the negotiation table with the demands made by the rebel side. Initially, the RUF demanded half of the cabinet portfolios, plus the substantive position of vice president, whilst the government side would only concede two seats. A stalemate was avoided by the advisory team, which came up with a formula of four cabinet positions, one of which would be at a senior level, and the chair of the Commission for the Management of Strategic Resources, National Reconstruction and Development (CMRRD). According to Nzongola-Ntalaja, it was the government of President Kabba that proposed that RUF-leader Foday Sankoh be offered the chair of the CMRRD, and the mediation committee added the icing on the RUF cake "with the rank, but not the title, of Vice President" (Nzongola-Ntalaja 2000, 50).

Perhaps the most outrageous of all concessions was the blanket immunity from prosecution accorded the RUF and its fighters. As one of the facilitators in the peace talks noted, it was surprising that after encouraging both sides to strike a peace deal, it was the UN and the international community that belatedly objected to the blanket immunity offered to the RUF. Again, it was late in the day that the UN offered to station peacekeeping troops in the country in preparation for a new national army, and it was not clear what role the government's ally, the CDF, would play in the maintenance of law and order in the country. In particular, the lack of any strong international stance in demanding retribution for human rights abuses in the war left Foday Sankoh and his fighters with a sense of triumphalism, steep in arrogance and political naivety throughout the negotiations. All they sought was the removal of all "foreign troops" from the country, meaning the Nigerian-led troops, so that they could overwhelm the weak and ineffective government fighters. They achieved this goal in May 2000, when the last of the ECOMOG forces left, and, following a blatant defiance against a UN restriction on his movement, Sankoh decided to visit South Africa, allegedly to trade in the country's diamonds, where he and his fighters embarked on a last *putsch* to capture the capital to ensure total RUF power in the country. Clearly, the Lomé chickens had come home to roost: by hurling a democratically elected government into negotiations with a bunch of armed thugs, the latter felt empowered to go the whole hog. It was this miscalculation that brought British paratroopers into the Sierra Leone war, as they formally came to evacuate British, Commonwealth, and European citizens from this West African theater of war. This resulted in the arrival of a superior force to confront the rebels, leading to their demise less than a year later.

Conclusion: Lessons of Lomé

Though peace has continued to reign in Sierra Leone, economic stagnation and poverty pose a major threat to the process of consolidating sustainable peace. As we have seen, the war was not precipitated by greed, but by grievances of a people who had seen their standards of living deteriorate through economic mismanagement, political incompetence, and kleptocratic rule. The accompanying woes to these policies were further fuelled by the conditionality of the structural adjustment programs imposed on the country by the International Monetary Fund and the World Bank, resulting in massive devaluation, cost-recovery programs, and massive reduction in government expenditure. The growing unemployment and poverty were major factors leading to conflict in the country. These are the issues that Lomé failed to address as the rebel leader was transformed from a warlord and the butcher of innocent Sierra Leoneans into a statesman and unelected vice president— the rogue that was put in charge of all the nation's minerals.

Nonetheless, the Sierra Leonean people have scored a number of victories: they have been able to face the issue of political succession in a way that has not been possible in almost fifty years as a nation. In 2007, relatively peaceful elections were conducted in a free and fair manner, leading to the defeat of the ruling Sierra Leone People's Party by the opposition, All Peoples' Congress, as democracy continues to develop, albeit in a tottering manner. Civil society continues to assert its independence, and a relatively vibrant press has returned to challenge political excesses, drawing attention to economic mismanagement and corruption. And even if civil society continues to be intimidated by the ruling party, they are not harassed in the manner of the *ancient régime* of Siaka Stevens and the old APC.

Furthermore, whilst their plight continues to be one of the worst in the world, the children of Sierra Leone are no longer positioned in Victorian terms—to be seen and not heard. The Child Rights Act of 2007 is now linked to those of the Convention on the Rights of the Child—adopted by the UN General Assembly on November 20, 1989, and its Optional Protocols on September 8, 2000—and the African Charter on the Rights and Welfare of the Child.

Many of the young people who gave up their weapons during the demilitarization process have now joined the large army of unemployed in the country. The global rise in food prices has had a major effect on consumers in Sierra Leone, a cereal consuming country. The government has been able to negotiate special delivery from India to tie it over until local projects for increasing domestic rice production start reaping benefits. Similarly, on women's issues, the new government of Mr. Ernest Koroma continues to promise changes, including the ending of the practice of female genital mutilation—a practice which impacts negatively on the health of women—which some 30 to 40 percent of Sierra Leone women have endured.

However, two further points are important to note at this juncture. The leaders of Sierra Leone must demonstrate that they have the political will to confront the challenges that the economy and society face, to rescue them from their long slumber, and to steer politics away from the tumultuous years of the old APC. Finally, Sierra Leone demands a period of soul-searching and value interrogation in order to exorcise the dysfunctional values that have brought the country to a period of prolonged conflict, and in order to seek values based on probity, diligence, personal and collective agency, as well as public spiritedness.

Notes

1. These words are associated with Stevens's much-feared deputy, S. I. Koroma, who claimed that if he did not win an election by the ballot box, then he could always win by declaring government candidates as returned unopposed, or win simply by getting the state-controlled broadcasting media to announce APC candidates as the winners (see Zack-Williams 1999).
2. See also Paul Collier (2007).
3. For a similar argument, which seems to be inadvertently sailing close to the "greed not grievance" argument, see Hoffman's (2004) otherwise interesting argument on the link between emergency institutions and increasing violence.
4. The phrase belongs to Mr. Eric Sesay, leader of the Bombali District Council, interviewed in February 2006 at the district headquarters in Makeni.

References

Abdullah, Ibrahim. 1997. Bush path to destruction: Origin and character of the Revolutionary United Front (RUF/SL). *African Development* Special Issue 22 (3–4): 45–76.

Abdullah, Ibrahim, ed. 2004. *Between democracy and terror: The Sierra Leone civil war*. Dakar, Senegal: Council for the Development of Social Science Research in Africa.

Abdullah, Ibrahim, and Patrick Muana. 1998. The Revolutionary United Front of Sierra Leone: A revolt of the lumpenproletariat. In *African guerrillas*, ed. C. Clapham, 172–93. Oxford: James Currey.

Abdullah, Ibrahim, and Ismail Rashid. 2004. Rebel movements. In *West African security challenges: Building peace in a troubled region*, ed. A. Adebajo and I. Rashid, 169–94. Boulder, CO: Lynne Rienner.

Bangura, Yusuf. 1997a. Reflections on the 1996 Sierra Leone peace accord. http://www.unsystem.org/ngls/documents/publications.en/voices.africa/ number8/9bangura.htm53k.

———. 1997b. Understanding the political and cultural dynamics of the Sierra Leone war: A Critique of Paul Richards' *Fighting for the Rain Forest*. *African Development* 22 (3–4): 117–48.

Cartwright, John. 1970. *Politics in Sierra Leone: 1947–1967*. Toronto: University of Toronto Press.

Collier, Paul. 2000. Doing well out of war: An economic perspective. In *Greed and grievance: Economic agendas in civil wars*, ed. M. Berdal and D. Malone, 91–112. Boulder: IDRC.

———. 2007. *The bottom billion: Why the poorest countries are failing and what can be done about it*. Oxford: Oxford University Press.

Fanthorpe, Richard. 2001. Neither citizen nor subject? "Lumpen" agency and the legacy of native administration in Sierra Leone. *African Affairs* 100 (400): 363–86.

Francis, David, ed. 2008. *Peace and conflict in Africa*. London: Zed Press.

Gberie, Lansana. 2000. First stages in the road to peace: The Abidjan process (1995–1996). *Accord: An international review of peace initiatives* (9): 8–25.

———. 2005. *A dirty war in West Africa: The RUF and the destruction of Sierra Leone*. London: Hurst.

Gbla, Osman. 2003. Conflict and post-war trauma among child soldiers in Liberia and Sierra Leone. In *Civil wars, child soldiers and postconflict peace building in West Africa*, ed. A. Sesay, 167–94. Ile-Ife: College Press.

Hoffman, D. 2004. The civilian target in Sierra Leone and Liberia: Political power, military strategy, and humanitarian intervention. *African Affairs* 103 (411): 211–26.

Kaplan, Robert. 1994. The coming anarchy: How scarcity, crime, overpopulation, and disease are rapidly destroying the social fabric of our planet. *Atlantic Monthly* (February): 44–76.

Keen, David. 2005. *Conflict and collusion in Sierra Leone*. Oxford: James Currey.

Lord, David. 2000. The struggle for power and peace in Sierra Leone. *Accord: An international review of peace initiatives* (9): 10–15.

Mohan, Giles, Ed Brown, Bob Milward, and Alfred B. Zack-Williams. 2000. *Structural adjustment: Theory, practice and impacts.* London: Routledge.

Musah, A. F. 2000. A country under siege: State decay and corporate military intervention in Sierra Leone. In *Mercenaries: An African security dilemma*, ed. A. F. Musa and J. K. Fayemi, 76–116. London: Pluto Press.

Nzongola-Ntalaja, George. 2000. Unpacking the Lomé Peace Accord. In *Sierra Leone: One year later*, ed. O. Oludipe, 1–46. CDD Strategic Planning Series. London: Centre for Democracy and Development.

Peters, K., and Paul Richards. 1998. "Why we fight": Voices of youth combatants in Sierra Leone. *Africa* 68 (2): 183–210.

Reno, William. 1995. *Corruption and state politics in Sierra Leone.* Cambridge: Cambridge University Press.

Richards, Paul. 1985. *Indigenous agricultural revolution: Ecology and food production in West Africa.* London: Hutchinson.

———. 1986. *Coping with hunger: Hazard and experiment in a West African farming system.* London: Allen & Unwin.

———. 1995. Rebellion in Liberia and Sierra Leone: Youth in crisis. In *Conflicts in Africa*, ed. O. Furley, 134–70. London: I. B. Taurus.

———. 1996. *Fighting for the rain forest: War, youth and resources in Sierra Leone.* Oxford: James Currey.

———. 2005. To fight or to farm? Agrarian dimensions of the Mano River conflicts (Liberia and Sierra Leone). *African Affairs* 104 (417): 1–20.

Sawyer, Edward. 2008. Remove or reform? A Case for (restructuring) chiefdom governance in post-conflict Sierra Leone. *African Affairs* 107 (428): 387–403.

Willer, David, and Judith Willer. 1973. *Systematic empiricism critique of a pseudoscience.* Englewood Cliffs, NJ: Prentice Hall.

Zack-Williams, Alfred. B. 1985. Sierra Leone 1968–85: The decline of politics and the politics of decline. In *Sierra Leone studies in Birmingham*, ed Peter K. Mitchell, 202–8. Birmingham: Centre of West African Studies, University of Birmingham.

———. 1990. Sierra Leone crisis and despair. *Review of African Political Economy* 49 (Winter): 22–33.

———. 1995a. Crisis and structural adjustment in Sierra Leone: Implications for women. In *Women pay the price: Structural adjustment in Africa and the Caribbean*, ed. G. T. Emeagwali, 53–63. Lawrenceville, NJ: Africa World Press.

———. 1995b. *Tributors, supporters and merchant capital: Mining and underdevelopment in Sierra Leone.* Aldershot: Avebury.

———. 1997. Kamajors, "Sobel" and the militariat: Civil society and the return of the military in Sierra Leonean politics. *Review of African Political Economy* 24 (73): 373–80.

———. 1999. Sierra Leone: The political economy of civil war, 1991–1998. *Third World Quarterly* 20 (1): 143–62.

———. 2001a. Child soldiers in the civil war in Sierra Leone. *The Review of African Political Economy* 28 (87): 73–82.

———. 2001b. The Ekutay: Ethnic cabal and politics ion Sierra Leone. In *The issue of political ethnicity in Africa*, ed. Ike E. E. Udogu, 125–48. Aldershot: Ashgate.

———. 2006. Child soldiers in Sierra Leone and the problems of demobilisation, rehabilitation and reintegration into society: Some lessons for social workers in war-torn societies. *Social Work Education: The International Journal for Social Work & Social Care Education, Training & Staff Development* 25 (2):119–28.

2

The Anatomy of Peacekeeping

ECOMOG's Role in the Sierra Leone Civil War

Joseph J. Bangura

Introduction

In the post-cold-war era, peacekeeping and peacemaking became a geopolitical phenomenon. The cold war and its subsequent arms race negatively affected Africa, making many of the continent's states fragile and susceptible to collapse. The consequence of the global arms race in Africa is that weak states became extremely vulnerable to disgruntled and dissident politicians, on the one hand, and warlords and strongmen, on the other. Between 1989 and 2000, much of Africa was engulfed in one conflict or another. Some Western nations that were active military or political players in Africa retreated to the background as warlords systematically ravaged their states. It became clear that the West was not interested in peacekeeping and peacemaking efforts, at least, in large measure, on the continent. The United Nations (UN), charged with the responsibility of keeping the peace, proved incapable of meeting such momentous tasks.

Although the UN succeeded in peacemaking in a few countries, the institution lacked the commitment and wherewithal to cope with the endless armed conflicts ravaging much of the continent. The inability of the UN to cope with such insurgent conflicts led to regional organizations assuming responsibility for keeping the peace in their different regions. Regional organizations such as the Southern African Development Community (SADC) and the Economic Community of West African States

Monitoring Group (ECOMOG), among others, enjoyed the advantage of proximity to the theaters of conflict (Maclean, Orr, and Shaw 1999; Adetula 2008). The involvement of these organizations in peacekeeping efforts reinforced the emerging notion of African solutions to African problems. As Jeffrey Herbst argues, "An African solution to African problems signals the end of the West's patronizing attitude to Africa and is another indication that the dream of the political independence for the countries south of the Sahara is becoming a reality." (Herbst 2000, 32)

This chapter examines ECOMOG's interventionist activity during the Sierra Leone Civil War. It argues that though ECOMOG was widely perceived as a peacekeeper and peace enforcer, its role in the Sierra Leone conflict is much more complex than we have been led to believe. In addition, the chapter addresses the following questions: Did ECOMOG's intervention in the Sierra Leone conflict save the state from collapse? Did ECOMOG's role facilitate the signing of the Lomé Peace Accord? Was ECOMOG a neutral intervenor and a professional peace broker in the Sierra Leone conflict? The chapter shows that while subregional organizations such as ECOMOG have played critical roles in maintaining peace in their regions, tension over hegemonic aspirations and regional power-politics continues to plague their activities. Finally, the chapter concludes by arguing that although ECOMOG engaged in abysmal human rights violations, it should be maintained as a standby regional force with the mandate to forestall state collapse usually triggered by rogue insurgents among ECOWAS member states.

ECOMOG and the Dynamics of Peacekeeping in Sierra Leone

A close examination of ECOMOG's role in the Sierra Leone conflict shows that it helped establish a propitious atmosphere that resulted in the signing of the Lomé Peace Accord between the government of Sierra Leone and the Revolutionary United Front (RUF) rebels, led by Foday Sankoh, in July 1999. To thoroughly understand the dynamics of ECOMOG's role, a succinct examination of the history behind its intervention is in order.

ECOMOG's intervention in the Sierra Leone conflict was aimed at ending a brutal civil war that resulted in the massive loss of lives and property. The Armed Forces Revolutionary Council (AFRC) coup in 1997 reversed Sierra Leone's democratic gains. The country became a complex emergency as chaos and anarchy consumed it. Like other complex emergencies in post-cold-war Africa, the AFRC in Sierra Leone looted the resources of the country, rendering the population desperate for humanitarian intervention, particularly as nonstate actors, such as nongovernmental organizations (NGOs) and UN agencies fled the country. Though the UN condemned the coup, it was, however, not interested in military intervention to resolve the impasse between the ousted Kabbah administration and the junta regime.

This standoffish attitude of the UN in resolving many civil conflicts in Africa through peacekeeping operations resulted in regional organizations fulfilling these roles, as Maclean, Orr, and Shaw (1999) argue. They note that while the UN undertook peacekeeping operations in conflict ridden regions and states in parts of the world, "recent peacekeeping missions have highlighted the range and complexity of issues and participants involved in attempting to solve conflict situations and to build or rebuild social and political structures in order to prevent the recurrence of future problems" (Maclean, Orr, and Shaw 1999, 130).

In addition, the collapse of the Liberian state in 1989 prompted the formation of ECOMOG by West African leaders, particularly when it became evident that the international community was not prepared to intervene. The decision to form a cease-fire monitoring group was taken by the Standing Mediation Committee at an ECOWAS summit in Abuja in 1990. Sierra Leone fully participated and supported the decision made at the summit. As a matter of fact, in 1990, Nigerian forces were based in Sierra Leone under a status-of-forces agreement, charged with the responsibility of supporting ECOMOG operations in Liberia. The forces were also charged with the mission to help President Joseph Momoh in "combating [sic] operations against the rebels and in training the national army" (Olonisakin 2008). In spite of the presence of Nigerian forces, a group of junior officers led by Captain Valentine Strasser overthrew the government of President Joseph Momoh in 1992 (Bangura 2009). Strasser established the National Provisional Ruling Council (NPRC) regime. After four years of NPRC rule, parliamentary and presidential elections were held, and Tejan Kabbah of the Sierra Leone Peoples' Party won the presidential election. He maintained the bilateral agreements with Nigeria signed by his predecessor, Joseph Momoh. In 1997, Nigeria agreed to train members of the Sierra Leone army and presidential guard. Ghana and Guinea also maintained small contingents in addition to the Nigerian troops (Berman and Sams 2000). It is clear that President Ahmed Tejan Kabbah entered into these arrangements because of the precarious security situation prevalent in the country, particularly as the RUF insurgency continued largely unabated at this point. The RUF controlled a significant portion of the country, including the all-important diamond-rich Kono District. Hence, President Kabbah was keen to have foreign troops in Sierra Leone, though he failed to renew the contract of mercenary troops. In addition, there was evident tension between the presidency and the national army (Bangura 1997). The

Sierra Leone Army apparently competed with local militias, such as the Kamajors, in defense of the country, a development that further deepened mistrust between the president and the national army. President Kabbah also publicly raised suspicion of plots to overthrow his government on numerous occasions in the national media, thereby justifying his reliance on Nigerian forces to protect his regime (Kabbah 1996; Mortimer 2000).

Notwithstanding this, junior officers of the army, led by Johnny Paul Koroma, overthrew the Kabbah administration in a bloody coup on May 25, 1997. The coup attracted national and international condemnation. Unscathed by the intensity of the gigantic fury expressed by foreign governments over their action, the coup leader invited the RUF rebels to join their ranks (Koroma 1997; Mustapha and Bangura, this volume).[1] Together, the RUF rebels and elements of the Sierra Leone Army formed the Armed Forces Revolutionary Council (AFRC), a regime that turned out to be one of the most brutal in the history of Sierra Leone.[2] In a radio broadcast, Major Johnny Paul Koroma outlined the reasons for the overthrow of the SLPP: the privileging of local militias over the national army in defense matters, the mortgaging of national security to Nigeria, and the failure to strike a peace deal with the RUF rebels (Koroma 1997).

The AFRC junta plunged the country into a state of interregnum as rebels descended on the capital city of Freetown in droves and flocked to other urban centers, wreaking unfathomable carnage on civilians. President Kabbah and his government fled to Guinea in self-imposed exile. Though in exile, the international community continued to recognize the Kabbah administration as the legitimate government of Sierra Leone. Many Sierra Leoneans at home and abroad vehemently opposed the AFRC through civil disobedience—a lethal and effective strategy—that played a role in undermining the junta.[3]

The overthrow of President Kabbah prompted a response from the Nigerian forces stationed in Sierra Leone. Their initial attempt to reinstate the president led to clashes with the junta regime. This did not dissuade the Nigerian government from increasing its troop levels and reinforcing their positions on the outskirts of Freetown. In fact, the Nigerian forces embarked on intermittent aerial bombardments of AFRC government positions, which led to civilian casualties, particularly as military targets were often missed. Such misdirected aerial bombardments by Nigerian forces attracted criticisms from human rights activists and supporters of the AFRC regime. It should also be pointed out that while Nigeria carried out these military strikes against junta positions in Freetown, such actions were not officially endorsed by ECOWAS as a body or by the United Nations Security Council. In short, many questioned Nigeria's military attacks on the AFRC junta in an attempt to reverse the coup. To blunt such criticisms, Nigeria characterized the intervention as an ECOMOG initiative. Clearly, ECOWAS did not authorize such unilateral military actions against a sovereign state by its military wing. Berman and Sams (2000) argue that "whereas in Liberia, Nigeria had sought . . . ECOWAS authorization prior to intervening, in Sierra Leone, Nigeria responded militarily first and sought ECOWAS approval only after it had intervened." In spite of the fact that some francophone ECOWAS countries criticized Nigeria's unilateral intervention in the Sierra Leone conflict, the Organization of African Unity (OAU), now African Union, ECOWAS and the UN strongly condemned the AFRC junta and demanded the reinstatement of the democratically elected government of President Kabbah. The United Kingdom, apparently in support of the exiled Kabbah government, sponsored a UN resolution, Resolution 1132. The resolution unequivocally supported ECOWAS efforts to reverse the coup and imposed sanctions on the AFRC regime if the regime failed to restore civilian rule. The resolution was adopted unanimously. Because there was no UN force in Sierra Leone to impose sanctions contained in Resolution 1132, ECOMOG forces received directives bearing the imprimatur of the UN to do so.

ECOMOG in Sierra Leone: The Debate

ECOMOG's intervention in the Sierra Leone conflict is the subject of intense scholarly discourse. Many theorists and security experts have debated the role of ECOMOG in the Sierra Leone conflict. Victor Adetula (2008, 9) notes, "A new awareness is growing in Africa about the role of subregional organizations in the prevention and management of conflicts." Adetula sees ECOMOG's role in West Africa as a link between "regionalism and collective security." He argues that West African leaders adopted a realist, rather than an idealist, approach toward solving the Sierra Leone and Liberian conflicts. Assensoh and Alex-Assensoh (2001), Adebajo (2004), and Clayton (1999), among others, praise the action of ECOMOG in intervening in the Sierra Leone conflict.

Conversely, scholars such as Berman and Sams (2000), Mortimer (2000), and others argue that the motives of ECOMOG's intervention in the Sierra Leone conflict were beyond peacekeeping. Berman and Sams (2000) note that the putative motivation of ECOMOG, particularly Nigeria, the force's biggest troop contributor and sponsor, was to use Sierra Leone as "pet project" to win international legal-rational legitimacy for the illegitimate Abacha regime. This is because Nigeria was the first to respond militarily to the crisis before seeking ECOWAS's approval. Mortimer (2000) views the activities of ECOMOG in Sierra Leone as a purely hegemonic exercise by Nigeria. Sympathizers of this view note that Nigeria's enthusiasm, under the military dictatorship of Sani Abacha, in intervening in the conflict was to entrench her role as the region's hegemon. In other words, critics note that Nigeria was neither a benign intervenor nor a disinterested peacekeeper in the Sierra Leone Civil War.

The literature on the role of hegemons in peacekeeping situations speaks to the fact that hegemons "will continue to do the intervening where, when and if [sic] it suits their own national interests" (Rotberg 2000, 12). Nigeria, as the regional hegemon, used ECOMOG to further its national interest. Similarly, in 1998, Senegal, a significant regional player, used ECOMOG to intervene in Guinea Bissau, under the guise of benign peacekeeping, after Brigadier-General Ousmane Mane launched an armed attack against President Joao Vieira. The Guinea Bissau coup was a worrying development to the government of Senegal, particularly when it was struggling to contain an ongoing insurgency in the Casamance region. In sum, Senegal's intervention in Guinea Bissau was also not officially sanctioned by ECOWAS.

Given the definitions of peacekeeping advanced by Rotberg (2000) and Kieh and Mukenge (2002), it can be argued that ECOMOG's role in the Sierra Leone conflict did not fit the traditional mode of peacekeeping. Rotberg defines peacekeeping as the act of sending peacekeepers "to a (usually) developing nation to prevent interstate [and intrastate] war, to reduce further hostilities between or among angry groups in a country, and generally to deter conflict" (2000, 1). He notes that the job of the peacekeeper is to prevent antagonists from killing each other. In an interesting theoretical work on conflicts in Africa, Kieh and Mukenge note that peacekeeping forces should intervene "in a conflict with an agreement of all or some of the parties" (2002, 16). Records show that ECOMOG did not obtain the consent of all warring parties in the Sierra Leone Civil War when it intervened in 1997 and 1998.

However, while the international community—including the UN—supported the reversal of the coup by ECOMOG, it is clear that ECOMOG leaders remained divided over the force's role in the conflict. Some West African leaders accused ECOMOG of unilateral action. Such criticisms forced the Nigerian leadership to press West African leaders for a full-scale military intervention by ECOMOG. After much lobbying by the Nigerian leadership and the Kabbah administration, ECOWAS agreed as a body to expand the role of ECOMOG in Sierra Leone. In particular, ECOWAS leaders mandated ECOMOG to assist in creating the right atmosphere, including the use of force, for the restoration of President Kabbah and his administration. Despite the adoption of this position by ECOWAS, tension engulfed the leadership of the West African body, as there was an apparent split over how ECOMOG forces should be used. Several French-speaking countries, particularly Senegal and Burkina Faso, criticized Nigeria for its domination of ECOMOG and for hijacking its mission. In many of these countries, the press also became very critical of Nigeria's hegemonic aspirations and "eternal quest for leadership" in the region (Mortimer 2000).

Some prominent Sierra Leoneans, such as Abbas Bundu, John Karefa-Smart, and ex-president Joseph Saidu Momoh, also challenged the legality of ECOMOG's intervention in the Sierra Leone conflict. In 1997, when ECOMOG forces attempted to reverse the coup against President Kabbah, these citizens objected to what they perceived as blatant interference in the internal affairs of Sierra Leone. They argued that the status-of-forces agreement signed between Sierra Leone and Nigeria—which Nigeria occasionally invoked when it came under blistering criticism—did not authorize the use of force in support of any government in power, including President Kabbah. Bundu, a former executive secretary of ECOWAS, played a critical role in the establishment of ECOMOG as a peacekeeping wing of ECOWAS. He therefore challenged the legality of using ECOMOG forces in siding with the Kabbah administration over the AFRC. In his major work on the subject, Bundu argued that Nigeria's intervention in Sierra Leone under the guise of ECOMOG was illegal (2001). In a series of radio broadcasts and discussions, he fiercely condemned and berated Nigeria for its flagitious meddling in Sierra Leone's internal affairs. It should be pointed out that through his actions and pronouncements, Bundu was perceived to be a supporter of the AFRC-RUF regime (Bundu 1997).

The former president of Sierra Leone, Major General Saidu Momoh, overthrown in a coup d'etat by junior officers of the Sierra Leone Army in April 1992, also lambasted the Nigerian involvement in the Sierra Leone conflict. In a British Broadcasting Corporation (BBC) interview, Momoh condemned what he believed was flagrant interference by Nigeria in the internal affairs of Sierra Leone. In addition, he argued that an armed intervention by ECOMOG in the Sierra Leone crisis would result in a bloodbath. One of my informants reminisced to me that the former president visited the Nigerian leadership in Abuja in an attempt to persuade them to pull back their forces from Sierra Leone. The Nigerian government turned down the request (Bangura 1997). The fact that there was so much vocal opposition within and outside Sierra Leone against ECOMOG's intervention in the conflict speaks to Kieh and Mukenge's point that traditional peacekeepers should intervene in a conflict only when all parties agree to such interventions. This is because theories of peacekeeping indicate that peacekeepers must demonstrate neutrality and impartiality. The major determinant of successful peacekeeping operations is the capacity of the peacekeepers to create an atmosphere conducive to peacekeeping. Sources indicate that ECOMOG did not meet this standard of peacekeeping. In fact, the UN resolution that followed the reinstatement of President Kabbah and his administration implicitly blamed ECOMOG forces for human rights abuses. Mortimer argues that Nigeria's offensive and dislodgment of the AFRC junta could be perceived as "reestablishment of a military protectorate" over Sierra Leone at the time it was reducing its troop presence in neighboring Liberia.

Despite the disagreements and opposition of the use of ECOMOG by Nigeria in Sierra Leone, in 1997, negotiations opened between ECOWAS and representatives of the AFRC junta in Conakry, Guinea, with the aim to end the impasse (ECOWAS 1997). The negotiations yielded positive results, with the junta agreeing to a cease-fire to be monitored by ECOMOG (Mustapha and Bangura and Zack-Williams, this volume). The agreement also indicated that UN peacekeepers or observers should replace ECOMOG forces. Sierra Leoneans and the international community hailed the Conakry agreement. However, the agreement was never fully implemented. The junta quickly reneged on key provisions of the agreement, particularly areas dealing with disarmament and demobilization of its combat forces. Such abjuratory acts by the junta provoked Nigerian anxiety and impatience. The Nigerian leadership pressed for a full-scale military intervention to oust the junta (Olonisakin 2008). Though Nigeria fretted about the need to reinstate President Kabbah and his administration in the wake of the junta's demission of its obligations under the Conakry peace agreement, sources indicate that the British and American governments furtively provided military aid and support to ECOMOG and the exiled Sierra Leone government. The British firm, Sandline, though it demonstrated subreption, came under heavy criticism for supplying weapons to ECOMOG in violation of a UN arms embargo imposed on Sierra Leone.

With the Conakry peace deal in jeopardy, ECOWAS continued to push for a diplomatic solution to the crisis. Despite such overtures of diplomacy, Nigerian forces, under the guise of ECOMOG, engaged in intermittent clashes with junta forces. Nigerian troops deployed at the Lungi International Airport embarked on aerial bombardment of Freetown, with bombs hitting civilian residential areas. Civilians became innocent victims of such aerial bombardments, resulting in civilian deaths and loss of property (Bangura 1997). In spite of the colossal loss of civilian lives, the Nigerian forces enjoyed relatively high support among the Sierra Leonean people, who determinedly refused to succumb to junta rule. However, clashes between junta forces and the Nigerians came to a head in February 1998.

Using ECOMOG as cover, Nigerian forces launched a full-scale offensive against junta positions on the grounds that its forces had been provoked. In a radio broadcast in February 1998, the Nigerian field commander, Colonel Maxwell Kobe (1998), announced the planned assault and ordered the

AFRC-RUF coalition leadership to yield power and vacate the capital city. After two weeks of intensive fighting, the Nigerian-led ECOMOG forces dislodged the AFRC-RUF coalition, compelling the torpid leadership, particularly Johnny Paul Koroma and Sam Bockarie, to flee the city.

The Intersection of Peacekeeping and Human Rights

It is worth pointing out that the routing of junta forces created more chaos than peace in Sierra Leone. With the swift defeat of the AFRC-RUF coalition forces, the country was gripped by an eerie state of interregnum: no government functionary filled the void created by the departure of Koroma and his forces. The ensuing chaos led to revenge killings by mobs with the complicity of ECOMOG forces. Supporters of the ousted Kabbah administration embarked on a killing spree, where perceived supporters of the routed junta regime described as "collaborators" were subjected to mob beatings and arson.[4] In fact, prominent politicians of the opposition party then, the All Peoples' Congress (APC), and religious figures deemed critical of the activities of Nigerian forces, such as Alhaji Musa Kabia and Sheik Mushtaba, among others, were burned alive and beaten to death by so-called supporters of the Kabbah administration. In all this, ECOMOG forces failed to provide security for many civilians, especially the maligned and suspected portion of the population. The breakdown of law and order and the string of revenge killings were triggered by lack of professionalism on the part of ECOMOG, on one hand, and the acrimonious statements made by a government-backed anonymous radio station, FM 98.1, based at Lungi, on the other. Messages from the radio broadcasts targeted AFRC-RUF supporters and sympathizers. Several of those named in the broadcasts became targets of revenge attacks. ECOMOG forces also embarked on the inhumane treatment of people described as "junta collaborators," as it carried out summary executions of rebel suspects and junta abettors. A gruesome case in point is the summary execution of a rebel suspect at the Kissy Road Cemetery in February 1998. The ECOMOG soldier, in the presence of a huge crowd of onlookers, shot dead the accused rebel suspect. In rationalizing his action, the soldier indicated that he killed the suspect because supporters of the Kabbah administration told him that the deceased acted suspiciously and he was therefore a "junta collaborator and sympathizer." Other incautious acts committed by ECOMOG forces during this period include harassing, scolding, and, on numerous occasions, buffeting innocent civilians at various checkpoints erected after the collapse of the AFRC regime. At the Aberdeen Road Bridge, for example, a Nigerian ECOMOG officer, nicknamed "Evil Spirit," harangued motorists and their passengers regardless of their status in society. His whimsical behavior forced many motorists and passersby to use alternative routes to get to Freetown (Bangura 1998). While the exiled Kabbah government quickly dispatched senior officials to help restore order in the country, it was rather too late for the helpless citizens who lost their lives in the hands of unruly mobs and unprofessional ECOMOG forces.

Nonetheless, ECOMOG and ECOWAS reinstated President Kabbah and his government in March 1998 at an aureate ceremony attended by West African heads of state. In the wake of its reinstatement, the Kabbah administration disbanded the Sierra Leone Army (SLA), retaining a few officers deemed loyal to it. ECOMOG forces replaced the SLA, essentially and practically putting the Nigerian-dominated force in charge of the national security of Sierra Leone.

Though ECOMOG was in charge of national security and securing peace, it quickly became clear that it was unable to secure peace in the country, as the AFRC-RUF coalition forces continued to wreak massive havoc on the countryside. In fact, on January 6, 1999, the AFRC-RUF coalition launched a deadly attack on Freetown, killing thousands of innocent civilians. In response, ECOMOG and civil militias launched a counteroffensive and, after two weeks of intense fighting, drove the rebels out of the city. Though the rebels lost the capital city, they controlled large parts of the interior of the country, killing innocent civilians. In the capital city where ECOMOG had a significant troop presence, militia groups and ECOMOG forces killed so-called rebel collaborators. Politicians of opposition parties, particularly the All Peoples' Congress, were detained without trial. A documentary critical of the activities of ECOMOG, *Cry Freetown*, was banned by the Kabbah administration from being aired in the country. The documentary details various human rights abuses carried out by ECOMOG forces. Testimonies before the Truth and Reconciliation Commission (TRC) also detailed numerous cases of human rights abuses carried out by ECOMOG and its militia allies (AfricaFocus 2004).

Conclusion

It can be argued that the successful signing of the Lomé Peace Accord in 1999 between the warring factions in the Sierra Leone civil war is attributable to ECOMOG's efforts in ousting the AFRC junta in 1998 and 1999. Clearly, ECOMOG's military triumph over the rebel forces weakened, and may have forced them to agree to a negotiated settlement of the conflict, subsequently leading to the signing of a peace accord. In other words, while the international community played an important role in getting the

Kabbah administration and the AFRC-RUF coalition to the negotiating table, it is apparent that the rebels would not have acceded to a peace deal if they had not been defeated on the battlefield. Other scholars disagree with this point of view, noting that there were no victors in the Sierra Leone conflict. They argue that both warring factions—the Sierra Leone government and the AFRC-RUF coalition—came under heavy pressure from the international community to negotiate a deal.

Despite the numerous human rights abuses carried out by ECOMOG and its allied forces, particularly the Kamajors, this chapter argues that the force should be maintained as a regional standby force, free from political interference or manipulations. ECOWAS should restructure and reorganize the force with all member states contributing troops. Such an action by all member states will help ECOMOG rise to the security challenges of the subregion, which will help achieve the goal of "African solutions to African problems" touted by the African Union. A clear case in point is the recent coup d'etat carried out by junior officers of the Guinean armed forces led by Captain Moussa Dadis Camara (International Crisis Group 2009; Kamara 2009). ECOMOG has not intervened militarily to stop the carnage perpetrated on the civilian population because the big powers within ECOMOG, particularly Nigeria, do not have a stake in the crisis. While Guinea's membership in ECOWAS has been suspended and the European Union has imposed sanctions, there is no standby force to implement the arms embargo, as was the case with Sierra Leone and Liberia.

In all, in spite of the professional failings of ECOMOG, its role in creating the conditions that led to the signing of the Lomé Peace Accord between the government of Sierra Leone—under the leadership of Ahmed Tejan Kabbah—and the Revolutionary United Front rebels should be appreciated and commended. Albeit Sierra Leone is still a postwar nation and not a postconflict state, as some erroneously claim, the successful implementation of substantial provisions of the Lomé Peace Accord helped make it possible for the holding of two successful democratic elections.

Notes

1. Corporal Tamba Gborie of the Sierra Leone Army announced the overthrow of the democratically elected Sierra Leone People's Party government on May 25, 1997. The coup plotters also broke the Pademba Road prison and freed many dangerous criminals.
2. The author, who taught African history at both Fourah Bay College and Milton Margai College of Education, witnessed these events. He, like other college professors, schoolteachers, thousands of civil servants, among others, withheld

their services in protest of the AFRC junta and demanded the restoration of the democratically elected government of President Kabbah.

3. Sierra Leoneans stoutly and vehemently opposed the AFRC junta through civil disobedience which proved extremely lethal in undermining the regime. While the international community is credited for the role it played in ending the war, the role the Sierra Leonean people played in sabotaging and thus, weakening the regime is sometimes overlooked by scholars.

4. This author witnessed many of these extremely gruesome killings in person.

References

Adebajo, Adekeye. 2004. ECOWAS: A retrospective journey. In *West Africa's security challenges: Building peace in a troubled region*, ed. Adekeye Adebajo and Ismail Rashid, 21–49. Boulder, CO: Lynne Rienner.

Adetula, Victor A. O. 2008. The role of sub-regional integration schemes in conflict prevention and management in Africa: A framework for a working peace system. In *The resolutions of African conflicts: The management of conflict resolution and post-conflict reconstruction*, ed. Alfred Nehema and Paul T. Zeleza, 9–21. Oxford: James Currey.

AfricaFocus. 2004. Sierra Leone: Truth and Reconciliation Commission report. *AfricaFocus Bulletin*, October 31. http://www.africafocus.org/docs04/sl0410.php.

Assensoh, A. B., and Yvette M. Alex-Assensoh. 2001. *African military history and politics*. New York: Palgrave Macmillan.

Bangura, Joseph J. 1997. Personal diary of events on the interregnum in Sierra Leone. Freetown, Sierra Leone.

———. 1998. Personal notes on the military clash between ECOMOG and Sierra Leone army. Freetown, Sierra Leone.

———. 2009. Understanding Sierra Leone in colonial West Africa: A synoptic socio-political history. *History Compass* 7 (3): 583–603.

Berman, Eric G., and Katie E. Sams. 2000. *Peacekeeping in Africa: Capabilities and culpabilities*. Pretoria: United Nations Institute for Security Studies.

Bundu, Abass. 1997. Speech given on national radio and television. *Sierra Leone Broadcasting Service*. Freetown, Sierra Leone.

———. 1998. The case against intervention. *West Africa* (June 30): 1039–40.

———. 2001. *Democracy by force: A Study of international military intervention in the conflict in Sierra Leone from 1991–2000*. London: Universal Publishers.

Cole, Desmond. 1998. Interviewed by Joseph Bangura. Tape Recording, June 17. Freetown, Sierra Leone.

Clayton, Anthony. 1999. *Frontiersmen: Warfare in Africa since 1950*. London: Routledge.

ECOWAS. 1997. The Conakry Peace Plan: *ECOWAS six-month plan for Sierra Leone, 1997–1998. The Sierra Leone Web*, October 23. http://www.sierra-leone.org/conakryaccord.html.

Government of Sierra Leone and the Revolutionary United Front. 1999. Peace agreement between Government of Sierra Leone and the Revolutionary United

Front. The Sierra Leone Web, June 3. http://www.sierra-leone.org/lomeaccord .html.

Herbst, Jerrey. 2000. African peacekeepers and state failure. In *Peacekeeping and peace enforcement in Africa: Methods of conflict prevention*, ed. Robert I. Rotberg and others, 16–33. Washington, DC: Brookings Institution Press.

International Crisis Group. 2009. Guinea: Military rule must end. Africa briefing no. 66, October 16. http://www.crisisgroup.org/~/media/Files/africa/west -africa/guinea/B066%20Guinea%20Military%20Rule%20Must%20End.ashx.

Kabbah, Alhaji Ahmad Tejan. 1996. Televised speech. *Sierra Leone Broadcasting Service*. Freetown, Sierra Leone.

Kelfala, Keita. 1996. Interviewed by Joseph Bangura. Tape Recording, August 8. Freetown, Sierra Leone.

Kieh, George Klay, and Mukenge I. Rousseau. 2002. *Zones of conflict: Theories and cases*. Westport, CT: Praeger.

Kobe, Maxwell. 1998. Speech given on the removal of AFRC-RUF forces in Freetown. *Sierra Leone Broadcasting Service*. Freetown, Sierra Leone.

Koroma, Johnny Paul. 1997. Speech given for overthrowing the Sierra Leone government. *Sierra Leone Broadcasting Service*. Freetown, Sierra Leone.

Kamara, Ahmed M. 2009. ECOWAS imposed arms embargo on Guinea. *Newstime Africa*, October 18. http://www.newstimeafrica.com/archives/2718.

Maclean, Sandra J., Katherine Orr, and Timothy Shaw. 1999. Teaching African peacekeeping, peacemaking, and peacebuilding. In *Great ideas for teaching about Africa*, ed. L. Mist Bastian and Jane L. Parpart, 129–39. Boulder, CO: Lynne Rienner.

Mortimer, Robert. 2000. From ECOMOG to ECOMOG II: Intervention in Sierra Leone. *In African in world politics: The African state in flux*, ed. John W. Habbeson and Donald Rothchild, 188–207. Boulder, CO: Westview.

Olonisakin, Funmi. 2008. *Peacekeeping in Sierra Leone: The story of UNAMSIL*. Boulder, CO: Lynne Rienner.

Rotberg, Robert I. 2000. *Peacekeeping and peace enforcement in Africa: Methods of conflict prevention*. Washington, DC: Brookings Institution Press.

3

The 1999 Lomé Peace Accord and Child Combatants

For Di People? For Di Pikin? Or for the International Community?

Robert Tynes and Clarke Speed

Approximately twenty thousand child soldiers were used during the civil war in Sierra Leone from 1991 through 2002 (Coalition to Stop the Use of Child Soldiers 2006). All sides recruited children—the Sierra Leone Army (SLA), the Revolutionary United Front (RUF), the Armed Forces Revolutionary Council (AFRC), and the Civil Defense Force (CDF). Children, some as young as seven, were forced to fight and commit acts of brutality, and numerous girls were raped and turned into "sex slaves" (Coalition to Stop the Use of Child Soldiers 2001). The 1999 Lomé Peace Accord acknowledged the role that children played in the civil war and dedicated a paragraph—"Article XXX: Child Combatants"—to the issue of demobilizing and reintegrating child combatants back into Sierra Leonean society. Even though the accord provided legal recognition of the problems caused by the war, the agreement between the Sierra Leonean government and the RUF was generally deemed a failure. Problems with the accord included giving away too much power to an untrustworthy RUF (Abraham 2004), a weak central government that lacked the leverage to implement the agreement (Alao and Ero 2001), too little attention paid to civil society needs and desires (Jusu-Sheriff 2004), and not enough recognition of the numerous factions and social institutions involved in the decade-long civil war (Bangura 2000).

The agreement may have lacked an awareness of the political complexities of the situation in Sierra Leone; nevertheless, it could be argued that, on the surface, many of the articles proposed progressive and democratic actions. Articles XI and XII proposed reinstituting elections and an electoral commission. Article VII, paragraph 14, proposed dedicating the country's gold and diamond revenues to rebuilding public education, the healthcare system, and compensating victims of the war. And, as noted, Article XXX initiated the demobilization and reintegration of child combatants. In recognition of the international norm against the use of child soldiers, the agreement attempted to mend a tear in the social structure of Sierra Leone that occurred during the civil war. As such, Article XXX of the agreement appeared to be a worthwhile and necessary gesture for peace. Indeed, the convictions of AFRC rebels by the Special Court for Sierra Leone, and the approval of a National Child Rights Bill in Sierra Leone, might be viewed as further extensions of the norm put forth by the Lomé accord to protect children (Human Rights Watch 2007; *Awareness Times* 2007). The international norm against child soldiers seemed to be taking hold in Sierra Leone.[1]

But did it really? This chapter will explore what effects Article XXX has had in Sierra Leone. For whom is it working? Are former child soldiers being demobilized and integrated back into the communities from whence they came, or are they being abandoned?

Despite the good intentions of the Lomé article, the concepts of reintegration and demobilization have mostly served the international community—foreign governments, the United Nations (UN), as well as numerous non-governmental organizations (NGOs)—and not necessarily the child soldiers themselves.[2] As Mustapha (2006) points out, the parties who utilized children in combat showed little enthusiasm for returning youth back to civilian life, and "demobilization of child soldiers was mainly the initiative of the international community, although the government of Sierra Leone had some institutional structures in place to deal with the issue" (Mustapha 2006, 57). Furthermore, many former child combatants are not returning to their rural roots, but rather are more likely to choose the city as home and to become contentious urban youth. Hence, Article XXX of the Lomé Peace Accord has not been fulfilled, but rather has created a shell of a norm that serves the international community and has yet to embed in Sierra Leonean society.

What the Lomé Document Proposes

The Lomé Peace Accord took on the task of fixing what had become a widespread problem during the civil war—the conversion of children into combatants. The accord addressed the issue in two ways. First, it approached the issue socially, attempting to transfer underage soldiers back into their role as children. Second, it set the practical ground rules for how to execute the combatant-to-pikin exchange. While previous agreements (the 1996 Abidjan Peace Agreement and the 1998 Conakry Peace Agreement) had dealt with bringing soldiers back into civil society, Lomé was the first peace accord to confront the problem of children in war.

The accord had a clear grounding in previous international norms concerning the treatment of children. In the preamble there is a direct connection is made with the international viewpoint that children should be seen as vulnerable, as well as with the norm that childhood is a precursor to adulthood. Additionally, according to the accord, the inherent fragility of children necessitates extra attention by the state. The accord takes on these assumptions by linking itself to the most important UN instrument for protecting children, by stating in the preamble: "Recognising the imperative that the children of Sierra Leone, especially those affected by armed conflict, in view of their vulnerability, are entitled to special care and the protection of their inherent right to life, survival and development, in accordance with the provisions of the International Convention on the Rights of the Child" (Lomé Peace Accord 1999).

By framing the issue as such, the accord empowers the state to become a caretaker, a role predominately held by family and clan. In effect, it deems the society's treatment of children as faulty. And, by pulling in the Convention on the Rights of the Child, the accord draws a line for childhood at the age of eighteen. This norm was initially accepted by the state of Sierra Leone in 1990, when the CRC went into effect.[3] Of note here is that instead of asserting Sierra Leonean social norms about children, the Lomé Peace Accord further reinforced the world view of the international community.

The other piece of the Lomé Peace Accord that directly pertains to children is "Article XXX: Child Combatants." It charges the government with the specific task of tending to child soldiers: "It shall, accordingly, mobilize resources, both within the country and from the International Community, and especially through the Office of the UN Special Representatives for Children in Armed Conflict, UNICEF and other agencies, to address the special needs of these children in the existing disarmament, demobilization and reintegration process" (Lomé Peace Accord 1999).

The first key point here is that the state would not be alone in resolving the problem. The international community (both intergovernmental organizations (IGOs) and, potentially, NGOs) would work with the government to return child soldiers back to childhood. The second key point is that the document laid out a clearly defined pathway back to childhood: disarm, demobilize, and reintegrate (DDR). Fulfillment of the accord for child combatants required completing all three of these steps. These three actions then become a means for measuring the success or failure of Lomé with regards to solving the child soldier problem.

The DDR tract is generally seen by the UN as "a process that contributes to security and stability in a post-conflict recovery context by removing weapons from the hands of combatants, taking the combatants out of military structures and helping them to integrate socially and economically into society by finding civilian livelihoods" (United Nations Disarmament, Demobilization and Reintegration [UNDDR] 2008). The approach applies to combatants of all ages, whether they are twelve or fifty. However, the UN does recognize the different needs of children. According to the UN, child soldiers are not just those underage boys and girls who fight.[4] The UN looks at a larger cohort of people eligible for reintegration programs, framing them as "children associated with fighting forces" (CAFF). This includes combatants, cooks, porters, and so forth, as well as "those who fled armed forces and groups (often considered as deserters and therefore requiring support and protection), children who were abducted, those forcibly married and those in detention" (UNDDR 2008). Expanding the definition of child soldiers to CAFF not only increases the number of children who should receive attention (thereby increasing the obligation for IGOs and states), but it also recognizes the complexity of conflicts where children are pulled into the fray.

When it comes to disarmament, the goal is simple: remove weapons from civilians and return power to the state. But this process is not just about dumping guns at designated checkpoints. Rather, this phase is supposed to involve collection of small arms and ammunition, documentation of what is collected, and the development of future small-arms management programs for the state (UNDDR 2008). Disarmament is not age specific and, in the case of Sierra Leone, the process provided monetary, not moral, incentives to whoever turned their gun in. The ramifications of this phase of the process will be discussed in the "Looking Local and Moving Up" section but, suffice it to say, it was a part of the Lomé agreement that was realized to varying degrees.

As for demobilization, the UN bestows special attention to young combatants, and encourages immediate action: "Child demobilization/release is very brief and involves removing a child from a military or armed group as swiftly as possible. This action may require official documentation (e.g., issuing a demobilization card or official registration in a database for ex-combatants) to confirm that the child has no military status, although formal documentation must be used carefully so that it does not stigmatize an already-vulnerable child" (UNDDR 2008). The point is to deconstruct the soldier and to create a new record of the child, in essence, to ritualize the transition out of civil war and into civil society, that is, to make the child soldier a child citizen. Demobilization should also ready the child for the next and last phase of the process—that of reintegration. Once a child is documented, they can then be monitored and resources can be allocated. Reintegration is the most complex phase of DDR, especially for children, as it involves "family reunification, mobilizing and enabling the child's existing care system, medical screening and health care, schooling and/or vocational training, psychosocial support, and social and community-based reintegration" (UNDDR 2008). Of the three components, reintegration is also the most essential, serving as a bridge back to civil society and as insurance against the return to grievance-based conflict. The Lomé promise of DDR was implemented, but there have been several shortcomings.[5]

Critiquing the Accord

Bangura (2000) and many others have argued that Lomé ignored the ground-level reality of civil-war-stricken Sierra Leone (see, for example, Abraham 2004; Alao and Ero 2001; Jusu-Sheriff 2004). Bright (2000) notes that "one of the basic weaknesses of the agreement at the outset was its failure to include all the parties, particularly the remnants of the SLA." Bangura sees the standard operating style of international negotiators as a prime reason for failure: "These often rely on conventional methods of conflict resolution: they start by recognizing the interests of all parties in a conflict; then they try to stabilize the behavior of the combatants; and later they work incrementally to achieve peace. Policy-makers, especially those with a bureaucratic mind-set, prefer policies that will not upset their routine activities even if—as was made all too clear with the predictable collapse of the Lomé Accord—those policies have repeatedly been shown to be wrong-headed" (2000, 575).

And most critics agree on the most glaring fault of the accord—that of legitimizing the RUF by granting it the right to become a political party and by giving Corporal Foday Sankoh an "absolute and free pardon" (Article III and IX, Lomé Peace Accord 1999). The ambiguous nature of the accord carried on into the implementation phase when President Kabbah appointed Sankoh and Johnny Paul Koroma of the AFRC to head the Sierra

Leone National Committee for Disarmament, Demobilization and Reintegration (NCDDR) and the Commission for the Consolidation of Peace (CCP) (Abraham 2004). In essence, the move gave two major instigators of child-soldier recruitment the authority to determine the future of underage combatants.

Leaving aside the social and cultural dynamics of the situation, one could also analyze the problem from a more structural, international law point of view. One could state that the provisions for child soldiers in the Lomé Peace Accord needed greater legalization. Increased legalization would increase the effectiveness of the accord. In this case, legalization refers to "a particular form of institutionalization [that] represents the decision in different issue-areas to impose international legal constraints on governments" (Goldstein and others 2001, 2). This definition is underpinned by the notion that greater institutionalization can translate into more effective regulation of behavior. In "The Concept of Legalization," Abbott and others (2001) present an explication of legalization as applied to international treaties. The three dimensions of legalization are obligation, precision, and delegation. Obligation means "states or other actors are bound by a rule or commitments" (17). Precision is explained as the "rules unambiguously define the conduct they require, authorize, or proscribe" (17). And finally, delegation is present when "third parties have been granted authority to implement, interpret, and apply the rules; to resolve disputes; and (possibly) to make further rules" (17).

Bangura (2000) and others are critical of the obligation aspect of the Lomé Peace Accord. The RUF is untrustworthy to begin with and can never be trusted. As Abraham (2004, 217–18) argues, the RUF was never interested in striking a peace agreement because they knew that "their terrorist monstrosities visited on the poor and innocent people continue to haunt them: what would be the guarantee against reprisal attacks from their respective communities and the country at large? . . . The conjuring tricks in Abidjan and Lomé were to buy time to push forward the original RUF agenda: capture state power through violence." The dimension of obligation was missing altogether.

Looking at the precision of the agreement with reference to child soldiers, it is extremely general and problematic. The document has three sentences that apply to children and child soldiers. The preamble frames them as vulnerable and entitled to protection under international law, and Article XXX states that the government should focus on the needs of child soldiers, and should "mobilize resources" internally as well as externally (from the international community) to help them through the DDR process. What those needs are (social, psychological, economic, perhaps) as well as what types of resources shall be utilized (money, counseling, food, shelter, perhaps) is not defined in the agreement. Article XXXI calls on the government to offer "free compulsory education" for twelve years, which might be viewed as fulfilling a long-term essential service for reintegrating child combatants. However, this is the full extent of the article. The assumption is either that schools will be back up and running—reinstalled to their former state previous to the civil war—or that a whole new system of education will be erected. In either case, a major grievance that contributed to the war—lack of education—is poorly envisioned. The educational system post-Lomé is far from revamped. And, if the goal was, at a minimum, to return schools to their former condition, then students have once again been short-changed. Education can still be considered a grievance.

Finally, the delegation dimension could be harshly attacked for allowing Sankoh and Koroma to be put in charge of the NCDDR. The idea of placing one of the initiators of the decade-long violence in charge of disarming Sierra Leone—someone who is also an accused war criminal—seems antithetical to peace-building. This could have been a disaster. The lack of involvement of Sankoh might be the reason why this provision in the accord provided some success, though. The agreement's declaration directing the government to handle the problem of child soldiers, with the help of international organizations such as UNICEF, has turned out to be one of the most productive aspects of the document. The fact that an IGO could step in and gain control of the process has rescued DDR. According to the Sierra Leone Truth and Reconciliation Commission (SLTRC) (2004, 332), UNICEF has been "the key agency providing care for demobilised Sierra Leonean children involved in the conflict," assisting with the DDR of 6,774 children. That total equals about 33 percent of the total number of child combatants from the war. UNICEF has worked on many other projects rebuilding education in the state, providing healthcare, and creating skills-training programs for former child combatants. Another branch of the UN, the United Nations Assistance Mission in Sierra Leone (UNAMSIL), has helped with outreach programs that encourage the inclusion of children in the peace-building process.

For its part, in 2001, the Sierra Leonean government instituted the National Commission for War Affected Children (NaCWAC). In 2002, NaCWAC began its mission "to provide the requisite environment for psychosocial recovery, and capacity building of war affected and other disadvantaged children, for expeditious reintegration into their families and communities" (Republic of Sierra Leone 2007, 7). This includes working on skills training and education for children who were affected by the civil war. The commission is also building "trauma healing centres" in several different areas of the country. The SLTRC is critical of NaCWAC, though, stating, "Laudable though these projects are, NaCWAC seems to have lost focus on the essence of its primary duties" (SLTRC 2004, 329). Given the key role that UNICEF (as well as UNAMSIL) has played in DDR, the lackluster performance of NaCWAC does not diminish the fact that the dimension of delegation has been sufficiently fulfilled. It appears that the former legacy of false promises (the obligation dimension) and the extremely generalized writing of the child soldiers articles (the precision dimension) did not hinder the ground-level implementation and realization of the basic idea of the treaty—to help children.

Despite the successes of the DDR program—that of returning security to the state and of disarming and demobilizing child combatants—it has come up short of its final goal: "Overall, while the two 'Ds' in DDR have been completed, young people say that the 'R'—the reintegration essential to uniting these components to construct recovery, reconciliation and a new beginning—remains distinctly lacking" (Women's Commission for Refugee Women and Children 2002, 1).

The problem, then, is not about the strengthening of institutions. As argued above, even if one was to make the document more obligatory, with all political factions involved becoming more "true to their words," that would not improve the situation. After all, the impediment to reintegration has not been the Revolutionary United Front, nor has it been a lack of commitment by the Sierra Leonean government, the international community, or the NGOs involved. Additionally, drafting more precise language in the treaty would not expedite the return of child combatants to their former homes. Describing exactly when, and in what manner, the children should be repatriated would be a fruitless endeavor.

As a consequence, greater legalization or institutionalization is not what is needed. Perhaps, instead, one should look beyond the political mechanisms involved, and include the social transformations that resulted from an eleven-year civil war in which a significant component of society—the role of children—was deliberately reconfigured. Many children in Sierra Leone were abducted and forced to fight, and others joined to avenge the government or rebel wrongdoings. In both cases, children acquired a cache of power that they had not previously held, and this empowerment, especially in a society where children are marginal beings, is not easily forgotten or relinquished. Hence, to ask a former child soldier to reintegrate and give up his or her power is to ask them to act irrationally.

A Different Theory: Collective Behavior

The problem of reintegration can be seen as a collective-action problem. How does a state mobilize child soldiers to return to their former place in society? Even though child soldiers are individuals who have been transformed into new social roles, they are also part of a larger group phenomenon. The assumption is that child soldiers want to return to their families and relatives but cannot do so on their own. Hence, moving them to the stage of collective action necessitates formal organization. As Olson (1965, 7) states, "Purely personal or individual interests can be advanced, and usually advanced most efficiently, by individual, unorganized action . . . But when a number of individuals have a common or collective interest—when they share a single purpose or objective—individual, unorganized action . . . will either not be able to advance that common interest at all, or will not be able to advance that interest adequately. Organizations can therefore perform a function when there are common or group interests, and though organizations often also serve purely personal, individual interests, their characteristic and primary function is to advance the common interests of groups of individuals." Helping former child soldiers find their homes and former "legitimate" place in a post-civil-war society can be seen as a public good—something that is deemed beneficial for the state and citizenry. Olson argued that collective action toward producing public good is hard to accomplish with large groups unless incentives are provided to the individuals involved. The benefit of taking action, of producing the public good, must outweigh the cost of cooperating. In other words, reintegration for child soldiers must be worth it.

The Lomé Peace Accord alone provides few incentives to produce a public good, other than a general notion of education and health care for all (Article XXXI) and the ideological power of reinstituting civil society. Nevertheless, the agreement did generate the creation of government bodies, such as NaCWAC and a network of IGOs and NGOs, to work on the problem. Despite the seemingly flimsy agreement, the result was a large group of people taking collective action in order to solve the problem of child combatants. The result, however, was that very few registered child combatants participated. According to the UN (2004), DDR in Sierra Leone was "widely considered a success that could be applied to other peacekeeping operations" (See II, 21). This assessment is at odds with findings of the 2003 report of the Sierra Leonean Ministry of Social Welfare, Gender and Children's Affairs' District Recovery Committee, which states, "Out of 3002 registered separated children outside the Western area, 532 were receiving, or had received community-based support (18%)" (Sierra Leone Information System 2003a) and "out of 3917 registered child soldiers outside Western area, 419 have received support (11%)" (Sierra Leone Information System 2003b). An Austrian judge on the UN-backed Special Court in Sierra Leone was critical of such poor reintegration results, stating, "It's wrong for donors to just demobilize (combatants) and then stop. You've only done half the job. You have to give them not only training, but also a job" (Murphy 2007). So, from Olson's collective action point of view, the incentives must not have been large enough to outweigh the costs for child soldiers, as it appears that only a little over 10 percent were actually connecting with the end points of the DDR process. It appears that the incentives were enticing enough for the government, IGOs, and NGOs, though. Funds flowed from the international donors into UNAMSIL and into government coffers. NGOs also benefited. This is not to say that the funding was unwarranted, but rather to convey that all these institutions had incentives for collective action. This stream of funding was essential to institutionalizing the reintegration effort. Nevertheless, why was the success rate so low? After all, the work on the ground was aimed and was providing a framework of incentives for former child soldiers. Still, full reintegration has not materialized.

The assumption is that if the right incentives are provided, that is, that the benefits outweigh the costs, collective action is more likely to occur. In the case of reconstructing Sierra Leone and deconstructing the child soldier role, failure and shortcomings could be blamed on poor incentives. These children are not being offered what they need to reinsert themselves back into society. And it is imperative that the most effective incentives are found if Sierra Leone wishes to reincorporate child soldiers back into society.

The dilemma is not resolved just by picking new incentives, though. The problem necessitates a deeper understanding of collective behavior. Collective behavior, according to Smelser (1971, 8), is "mobilization on the basis of a belief which redefines social action." Here, "belief" can be equated with Olson's "common or collective interest." In Sierra Leone, there are two separate entities that are, or are trying to be, mobilized: the Sierra Leonean government-IGO-NGO nexus and child soldiers. The government-based group is mobilizing around the belief that children should not be soldiers, and if they do become combatants, then they should be returned to their previous role as children. The government hopes to redefine wartime social action, which empowered youth both physically and politically. The reactive social action by the government reframes child soldiers as children—people with less agency. The other group, child soldiers, however, does not necessarily adhere to the belief of reintegration. Many individuals within the group either want to maintain their newly gained political power or transform it into employment or education. Some may want to return to their families and villages, but certainly not all. Many families have not accepted ex-child soldiers back, asserting that the children are dangerous, which is one of the reasons why the RUF used children to commit atrocities. The tactic deconstructed the family, instilled fear, and severed community attachments. The RUF understood the threat that reintegration posed for their troops, so they provided "a major disincentive to do so" (Gislesen 2006, 34). Girl soldiers are even less likely to reintegrate, as they have been further stigmatized by acts of rape. So even though there is a force of IGOs, NGOs, and government institutions working to reinstitute children into civil society, the ex-combatants themselves are not necessarily moving toward that same goal.

Examining the core elements of social action, according to Smelser (1971), reveals why this separation into two different mobilizing groups has occurred. There are four basic components of social action: (1) values, (2) norms, (3) mobilization of energy to achieve goals, and (4) the situational facilities that are utilized to achieve goals (Smelser 1971, 24). Smelser goes on to explain that values are "the most general statements of legitimate ends which guide social action" (25); they provide the "criteria for judging the legitimacy or illegitimacy of whole classes of behavior" (26). Values are the beginning foundation for all social action. Norms are the next level of movement toward social action: "They specify certain regulatory principles which are necessary if these values are to be realized" (27). Norms can be formal laws or unspoken rules for behavior used by groups for social control. The third component, mobilization of energy to achieve goals, is when action becomes organized and more apparent. The specifications of social action are realized, such as "who will be the agents in the pursuit of valued ends, how the actions of these agents will be structured into concrete roles and organizations, and how they will be rewarded for responsible participation in these roles and organizations" (27). The final component of social action, that of situational facilities, refers to "the means and obstacles which facilitate or hinder the attainment of concrete goals in the role of organizational context" (28). Situational facilities are the structural realities related to why a group will or will not mobilize to social action.

As discussed above, the two groups involved in child combatant reintegration—the governmental nexus and the child soldiers—differ at the level of value. Hence, the core discrepancy starts at the beginning of social action. This is important because, as Smelser notes, the whole movement toward collective behavior is value-added. This means that each level "is a necessary condition for the appropriate and effective addition of value in the next stage. The sufficient condition for final production, moreover, is the combination of *every* necessary condition, according to a definite pattern" (1971, 14). So if there is difference in values between two groups, they must necessarily travel down different paths toward social action. Even if: (1) former child soldiers engage in the norms instituted by the government nexus—norms legally created by the Lomé treaty; (2) they participate in programs set up by the state or by IGOs or NGOs, demobilization, disarmament, and relocation to former homes; or (3) situational facilities, such as funding for programs, are continually replenished, the social action outcome for child soldiers has to diverge from the social action of the governmental nexus. The difficulty is that values are easily underobserved and underanalyzed, which appears to be the case in post-civil-war Sierra Leone. A prime example of this dynamic is provided by Hoffman (2003) in his description of Sierra Leoneans passing through the Bo disarmament center in 2001. He observed how children were often encouraged to pass themselves off as adults, and they willingly did so because "while child ex-combatants received rehabilitation, adults received direct material rewards. Children who could be snuck through brought benefits to their parent or patron, the latter often the commander in whose care a child was placed in by family or community" (Hoffman 2003, 300). The UN DDR wanted children to rehabilitate, but the child wanted to fulfill his or her neopatrimonial value system; hence, guns for money, and not rehabilitation, was the preferred collective behavior choice.

Looking Local and Moving Up

The problems inherent in the Lomé accord operate on both cultural and structural levels. Culturally, there are some basic differences in how childhood is conceived. According to philosopher David Archard (2004, 39), the modern, Western view is that "childhood is a stage or state of competence relative to adulthood. The ideal adult is equipped with certain cognitive capacities, is rational, physically independent and autonomous, has a sense of identity, and is conscious of her beliefs and desires, and thus able to make informed free choices for which she can be held personally responsible." The implication is that achieving adulthood means gaining agency. Sierra Leonean culture recognizes a similar procession from childhood to adulthood, most notably through initiations conducted by secret societies, such as Poro and Sande. The process teaches them social norms and rituals, and empowers them, allowing them to become soldiers, if needed.

Even though the Sierra Leonean norm marks puberty as the time when children become eligible for adulthood, similar to Western notions of maturity, the exact age is less important. In fact, boys and girls will never be viewed as adults nor viewed as eligible to fight in wars unless they go into the bush. This applies no matter how old they are—thirteen, twenty, or fifty years of age. The Sierra Leonean passage out of childhood was also seen as malleable during the civil war. CDF leader Chief Hinga Norman said that recruiting children for combat became an initiatory and civilizing process: "A lot of these kids witnessed the slaughter of their parents and were so traumatized that they were living like beasts in the bush. We had to catch them and bring them back into the fold as human beings" (as quoted in Hoffman 2003, 301). In contrast, the CRC delineates a specific age, fifteen, as the sole determinant for when a state is permitted to recognize a person as a legitimate combatant, that is, one who has the right to bear arms. The international initiation, then, becomes a birth date or structural mark.[6] A similar discrepancy over childhood demarcation also appears in the reintegration process. For example, girls in West Africa are viewed as adults after they give birth to their first child. During the war, many girls who were raped and became pregnant were considered to have passed into adulthood. After the war, returning to their families to assume a more submissive role was a complicated process, for "neither the girl soldier nor the parents would think it appropriate for her to be unified as a 'child'—she ought to establish a home for herself and her children" (Gislesen 2006, 36). In this manner, a girl can become an adult at age fifteen or age twenty.

Also of importance is the difference between the Western assumption that "the modern child is an innocent incompetent who is not but must become the adult" (Archard 2004, 50), and the Sierra Leonean premise that even though children may be socially insignificant, they may carry potential danger, or "concealed power." This is especially true when children are perceived as "liminal beings between the world of animality and madness" (Ferme 2001, 198).The Sierra Leonean view is not that children are vile or Hobbesian, but rather that they have access to multiple public and private domains. They have not cultivated "social values of shame and respect" as well as a connection with their ancestors, which would help regulate the power that they have access to (199). This belief is echoed by combatants in their explanation for why children make good fighters: "They are uninhibited by moral concerns" (Hoffman 2003, 301). Unfortunately, this cultural belief can become a circular, self-fulfilling prophecy for ex-child combatants. One boy who was not reaccepted by his father said, "When I came to Freetown, I tried to stay with my father . . . he rejected me and now I am staying in the streets. He said that he is no longer my father because I was a rebel . . . I tried to explain to him that it was not my fault . . . but he could not listen to me. I am now a chain smoker . . . I smoke cigarettes, cannabis sativa and have sex with prostitutes everyday . . . I even drink alcohol" (SLTRC 2004, 320). The father's actions are certainly not the desired response that DDR programs aim for, but the father's response could be read as a story about him trying to shame the child and instill social values that were taken away during the war. The rereading of this narrative is not meant to justify the father's rejection of the child, but rather to illustrate the complex cultural dynamics at play. One could see it as a story of rational actions taken by the father—he was protecting both his family's lives and his own. Alternatively, the story could be viewed as a culturally aligned form of reintegration in which shaming is important. The question then becomes, how does one include Sierra Leonean moral structures in the DDR process?

Neither the Western nor West African view of childhood prohibits caretaking by the society; however, the different views do affect the perceptions of, and methods for, reintegrating child combatants back into the local context. The IGOs took on an almost parenting role, first, by dictating the rules for the return of childhood to Sierra Leone, and second, by not including the existing cultural structure. Mustapha (2006) is critical of the exclusion of local and traditional communities from the reintegration process. He asserts that even when international donors funded Sierra Leonean civil society organizations, they usually supported those groups based in Freetown. Unfortunately, "these groups were expected to organize communities in which they had never lived" (Mustapha 2006, 62). While this may, from the Western point of view, seem like the most expedient way of distributing public goods, it ignores the fact that a large percentage of the child combatants came from rural areas. So, for instance, when it came to skills training, many children were taught skills such as "mechanics and driving . . . [which] would only be useful in an urban environment" and would not be applicable to the agricultural-based communities that they were supposed to return to (Gislesen 2006, 47).

The lack of cultural awareness on the part of UNAMSIL during the disarming phase also fueled preexisting negative views about how politics works and reinforced age-old structures of dominance: "The young combatants and excombatants of Sierra Leone tend to see the spoils of modernity going to identifiable actors on the local, national and international scene: the elders and elites favoured first by colonial powers, then by postcolonial strategies of extraversion, and now by multinational NGOs, corporations, and the UN" (Hoffman 2003, 304). During the DDR process, former war commanders were given prominent roles in the disarmament phase, resulting in corruption. According to Human Rights Watch (2005), regular payoffs to commanders for DDR cards were a common occurrence. If UNASMIL had been more attentive to the problems of patronage that led up to the war, they might have exhibited greater oversight in the distribution of goods and might not have given commanders carte blanche control. Instead, "pa-ism" was reestablished, which, to a former child soldier, meant that nothing had changed; and, if nothing had changed after the war, then the incentive to reintegrate was lessened. After all, it was the same system of "connectocracy" that had kept many youths disempowered and undereducated: "Most youths could never fulfill their ambitions because they were not "connected" to the political system (SLTRC 2004, 347).

One of the most glaring problems of the DDR that was not accounted for in the Lomé peace agreement was the neglect of women. The forgetting of girl soldiers became glaringly evident in the DDR process. According to the SLTRC (2004), about 30 percent of child soldiers were girls, but only 8 percent of them received any benefit from the DDR. Further, many women did not have guns, so they were not seen as ex-combatants even though they were abducted, raped, forced into "bush marriages," and required to cook and act as porters (Women's Commission for Refugee Women and Children 2002). The structure of the Lomé-appointed DDR process reinforced the cultural bias of ignoring women. As the SLTRC (2004, 240) notes, it is already an established "inclination not to educate girl children" in the northern and eastern parts of the country, so ignoring girl combatants in the reintegration further concretizes a cultural bias.

What Can Be Done?

If the promise of the Lomé Peace Accord has not been fulfilled, then what can be done now and in future agreements? On a theoretical level, the goal of a peace agreement should be to build a structure that can rechannel the power gained by child soldiers into productive, civil-society-strengthening projects. As it stands, the Lomé Peace Accord is premised on the myth that time is reversible—that somehow child soldiers can rewind history and return to their previous place in childhood. This is impossible, and yet the concept of reintegration seems to rely on that assumption. The child in Sierra Leone has become politicized and political, and even if former child combatants give up their guns, they will never be able to relinquish the wisdoms they learned in war.

The idea that reintegration is simply the task of reuniting children with their families and providing them with skills training seems to be dissipating, though. While this method may have been a cultural norm for the West, Sierra Leonean communities are turning away from DDR and toward traditional healing processes that incorporate "local belief systems or religious rituals held to rid the former child soldiers of evil, and sacrifice rituals to appease the ancestors (Gislesen 2006, 40). NGOs, such as Save the Children, no longer use the international DDR template in Sierra Leone, nor do they even label the former fighters as "ex-child soldiers." Instead, they focus on the local context and the needs of "communities of vulnerable children"—needs that include schools, sports venues, and jobs.[7] Local communities are also starting to commit to reintegration. In

January of 2008, the people of the Kailahun district publicly declared that they would accept their "brothers and sisters" who had once fought with the RUF back into the community (United Nations Integrated Office in Sierra Leone 2008).

Ultimately, the most salient need for ex-child combatants remains reempowerment. The civil war followed and exploited the breakdown of economic and educational opportunities. The result was a future that could not guarantee that the child would become an adult in a civil society. Instead, the war empowered the child by taking away his or her moral bearings (the community and family) and replacing these grounding norms with the culture of armies and killing and immediate gains (life, limb, and food). The task of any future work in Sierra Leone should be to reinstitute agency for these children. But again, the prewar family may not be the best, most powerful place to return. As McIntyre (2002) states, "Answering to African children means looking beyond the traditional areas of health, education and social services. It means developing a broad range of policies that take into account the burden of caring for demographically young populations, and managing their political engagement productively when true accountability cannot be enforced at the polls." After all, democracy might not always be in place, but that does not mean that children must become soldiers again.

Naturally, the situation in Sierra Leone is extremely complex and will take many years to resolve, and peace agreements such as Lomé will never be able to address and remedy all the problems that result from war. Nevertheless, when it comes to child combatants, provisions for DDR and educational rebuilding necessitate greater awareness of the local context that the articles will be applied to. In the case of Sierra Leone, disarmament and demobilization are not equal with reintegration. Reintegration involves a much more complicated web of norms and requires a more detailed set of incentives that will facilitate the movement of children into civilian life. Similarly, and especially because it was a major grievance before the war, educational deficiencies deserve much more than a sentence or two. Granted, the Lomé Peace Accord was the first to openly address the problem of child combatants. The deficiencies in the accord should be heeded, though, so that in the future, international remedies for child soldiers will actually make life better for children.

Notes

1. The United Nations Development Programme states that it has helped almost seven thousand child combatants disarm and demobilize. Reintegration, however, has not been as successful (Kaldor and Vincent 2006).
2. Some observers note that the agreement itself was drafted and pushed forward by the United States (Alao and Ero 2001).
3. Article 1 of The United Nations' 1989 Convention on the Rights of the Child (CRC) sets the age of a child as anyone under eighteen years old, and Article 38.3 sets the limit for states enlisting children into combat: "States Parties shall refrain from recruiting any person who has not attained the age of fifteen years into their armed forces. In recruiting among those persons who have attained the age of fifteen years but who have not attained the age of eighteen years, States Parties shall endeavour to give priority to those who are oldest" (United Nations 1989). The CRC entered into force in 1990, and the Sierra Leone government became a party to the agreement in that same year.
4. The minimum age for State recruitment of citizen changed from 15 to 18 years of age with the adoption of the Optional Protocol to the Convention on the Rights of the Child on the involvement of children in armed conflict in 2000 (United Nations High Commissioner for Human Rights 2002). This change, however, was made after the signing of the Lomé agreement.
5. An earlier agreement, the Abidjan Peace Accord (1996), set forth a DDR plan, but it did not outline a specific plan for child combatants, nor did the Economic Community Of West African States (ECOWAS) Conakry Peace Accord (1998). The Lomé peace agreement was the first accord to specifically address the need for DDR of children in Sierra Leone.
6. The SLTRC notes that the law of Sierra Leone, "defines a child as a person under the age of 14 years and a young person as a person who is above 14 years and under the age of 17 years" (2004, 247). While this may appear to align with the international norm, the law is actually a later permutation of the British tradition of justice, first acquired when the Sierra Leone was under colonial rule.
7. Personal correspondence with Save the Children UK representative, January 2008.

References

Abidjan Peace Accord. 1996. *Peace agreement between the government of the Republic of Sierra Leone and the Revolutionary United Front of Sierra Leone (RUF/SL)*. http://www.sc-sl.org/abidjanaccord.html.

Abbott, Kenneth W., Robert O. Keohane, Andreas Moravcsik, Anne-Marie Slaughter, and Duncan Snidal. 2001. The concept of legalization. In *Legalization and world politics*, ed. Judith L. Goldstein, Miles Kahler, Robert O. Keohane, and Anne-Marie Slaughter, 17–36. Cambridge, MA: MIT Press.

Abraham, Arthur. 2004. The elusive quest for peace: From Abidjan to Lomé. In *Between democracy and terror: The Sierra Leone civil war*, ed. Ibrahim Abdullah, 198–219. Dakar, Senegal: Council for the Development of Social Science Research in Africa.

Alao, Abiodun, and Comfort Ero. 2001. Cut short for taking short cuts: The Lomé peace agreement on Sierra Leone. *Civil Wars* 4 (3): 117–34.

Archard, David. 2004. *Children: Rights and childhood*. London: Routledge.

Awareness Times. 2007. Sierra Leone Approves the National Child Rights Bill. June 8.

Bangura, Yusuf. 2000. Strategic policy failure and governance in Sierra Leone. *Journal of Modern African Studies* 38 (4): 551–77.

Bright, Dennis. 2000. Implementing the Lomé peace agreement. http://www.c-r.org/our-work/accord/sierra-leone/implementing-lome.php.

Coalition to Stop the Use of Child Soldiers. 2001. *Child soldiers global report 2001*. http://www.child-soldiers.org/document_get.php?id=1262.

Coalition to Stop the Use of Child Soldiers. 2006. *Call for action on working with child soldiers in West Africa*. http://www.child-soldiers.org/document_get.php?id=1152.

Economic Community Of West African States (ECOWAS). 1998. *The Conakry Peace Accord*. http://www.sierra-leone.org/conakryaccord.html.

Ferme, Mariane. 2001. *The underneath of things*. Berkeley: University of California Press.

Gislesen, Kirsten. 2006. A childhood lost? The challenges of successful disarmament, demobilisation and reintegration of child soldiers: The case of West Africa. *Norwegian Institute of International Affairs* Paper 712. Oslo: Norwegian Institute of International Affairs.

Goldstein, Judith L., Miles Kahler, Robert O. Keohane, and Anne-Marie Slaughter. 2001. Introduction: Legalization and world politics. In *Legalization and world politics*, ed. Judith L. Goldstein, Miles Kahler, Robert O. Keohane, and Anne-Marie Slaughter, 1–16. Cambridge, MA: MIT Press.

Hoffman, Daniel. 2003. Like beasts in the bush: Synonyms of childhood and youth in Sierra Leone. *Postcolonial Studies* 6 (3): 295–308.

Human Rights Watch. 2005. Youth, poverty and blood: The lethal legacy of West Africa's regional warriors. *Human Rights Watch Reports* 17(5). http://www.hrw.org/reports/2005/westafrica0405/index.htm.

———. 2007. *Sierra Leone: Landmark convictions for use of child aoldiers*. http://www.hrw.org/english/docs/2007/06/20/sierra16214.htm.

Jusu-Sheriff, Yasmin. 2004. Civil society. In *West Africa's security challenges: Building peace in a troubled region*, ed. Adekeye Adebajo and Ismail Rashid, 265–90. Boulder, CO: Lynne Rienner.

Kaldor, Mary, and James Vincent. 2006. Case study Sierra Leone: Evaluation of UNDP assistance to conflict-affected countries. http://www.undp.org/evaluation/documents/thematic/conflict/SierraLeone.pdf.

Lomé Peace Accord. 1999. Peace agreement between the government of Sierra Leone and the Revolutionary United Front of Sierra Leone. http://www.sierra-leone.org/lomeaccord.html.

McIntyre, Angela. 2002. Reinventing peace: Challenges for a young continent. *African Security Review* 11(3). http://www.iss.co.za/ASR/11No3/McIntyre2.html

Murphy, Peter. 2007. Help Sierra Leone's child soldiers more, UN judge says. Reuters, November 30. http://africa.reuters.com/wire/news/usnL30457322 .html.

Mustapha, Marda. 2006. The use of child soldiers in the Sierra Leone conflict: Implications for democracy in post-conflict Sierra Leone. *Journal of African Social Sciences & Humanities Studies* (Winter): 43–69.

Olson, Mancur. 1965. *The logic of collective action: Public goods and the theory of groups.* Cambridge, MA: Harvard University Press.

Republic of Sierra Leone. 2007. *Report on the implementation of the optional protocol to the Convention on the Rights of the Child on the involvement of children in armed conflicts.* http://huachen.org/english/bodies/crc/docs/AdvanceVersions/ CRC.C.OPAC.SLE.1.doc.

Sierra Leone Information System. 2003a. Percentage of separated children receiving community support. *ReliefWeb*, June 2003. http://www.reliefweb.int/rw/ fullmaps_af.nsf/luFullMap/10BB9C5F6D9DEE1C85256DCF006CB4A8/$File/ slis_SepChldrn_sle0603.pdf?OpenElement.

Sierra Leone Information System. 2003b. Percentage of child soldiers receiving community support. *ReliefWeb*, June 2003. http://www.reliefweb.int/rw/ fullMaps_Af.nsf/luFullMap/E25E830D1190D62285256DCF006C4CF5/$File/ slis_ChldSldr_sle0603.pdf?OpenElement.

Sierra Leone National Committee for Disarmament, Demobilization and Reintegration. 2000. *Information Bulletin, Freetown.* http://www.worldbank.org/afr/ afth2/crrp/bulletin8-9.html.

Sierra Leone Truth and Reconciliation Commission (SLTRC). 2004. *Witness to truth: Report of the Sierra Leone Truth and Reconciliation Commission.* http:// www.trcsierraleone.org/drwebsite/publish/index.shtml.

Smelser, Neil J. 1971. *Theory of collective behavior.* New York: Free Press.

United Nations. 1989. *Convention on the Rights of the Child.* http://www.unhchr.ch/ html/menu3/b/k2crc.htm.

United Nations Disarmament, Demobilization and Reintegration. 2008. *IDDRS 1.20 glossary and definitions.* http://www.unddr.org/iddrs/01/20.php.

United Nations High Commissioner for Human Rights. 2002. *Optional protocol to the Convention on the Rights of the Child on the involvement of children in armed conflict.* http://huachen.org/english/law/crc-conflict.htm.

United Nations Integrated Office in Sierra Leone. 2008. Kailahun opens door to ex-combatants. *UNIOSIL Review of Sierra Leone Media Reports.* Available at: http:// appablog.wordpress.com/2008/02/02/review-of-sierra-leone-media-reports-52/.

Women's Commission for Refugee Women and Children. 2002. Disarmament, Demobilization and Reintegration, and Gender-based Violence in Sierra Leone. Excerpts from *Precious resources: Adolescents in the reconstruction of Sierra Leone.* http://www.womenscommission.org/pdf/sl_ddr03.pdf.

4

Shifting Priorities in Child Protection in Sierra Leone since Lomé

Susan Shepler

In the field of international struggles for the protection of children affected by war, there are many "firsts" in the Sierra Leone case. The accord signed in Lomé was the first African peace accord to specifically mention the reintegration of former child soldiers. The United Nations Mission in Sierra Leone (UNAMSIL) was the first UN peacekeeping force to include a child protection officer. The Special Court for Sierra Leone (SCSL) was the first international tribunal to convict individuals for war crimes for conscripting and enlisting children. Does all of this mean that Sierra Leoneans were particularly concerned about the rights of children? Or does it show that Lomé happened at a critical time in the progress of international child protection discourse and practice? What are the implications of the unprecedented focus on child rights for the postwar nation?

In this chapter, I will explain the centrality of child protection to postwar Sierra Leone by investigating the space at the intersection of local concerns and the international human rights regime.[1] I will begin by explaining each of the "firsts" I introduced in the introductory paragraph in greater detail. In addition, I will discuss the question of whether the various child protection activities for war-affected youth originated from inside or outside Sierra Leone, or from a complicated combination of the two. Next, I will look at various trends in child protection during the decade in question, and explain how those trends played out in programming in the Sierra Leone context. Finally, I will briefly analyze the state of child protection in Sierra Leone today, and introduce some tentative conclusions about fostering local constituencies for children and youth.

Firsts in Child Protection for Children Affected by War

Lomé was the first peace agreement to specifically mention the reintegration of former child soldiers. Specifically, "Article XXX: Child Combatants" states, "The Government shall accord particular attention to the issue of child soldiers. It shall, accordingly, mobilize resources, both within the country and from the International Community, and especially through the Office of the UN Special Representative for Children in Armed Conflict, UNICEF and other agencies, to address the special needs of these children in the existing disarmament, demobilization and reintegration processes" (Lomé Peace Accord 1999). From the language of the article, it is clear that the expertise required for addressing this issue was understood to be in the realm of primarily international actors. The UN was also interested in child protection in a new way. The UN peacekeeping mission to Sierra Leone was the first UN peacekeeping mission to include a child protection officer. According to the report of the Sierra Leone Truth and Reconciliation Commission (SLTRC), "UNAMSIL was the first UN peacekeeping mission to have had staff deployed specifically in the fields of child protection and child rights issues directly in the office of its Special Representative of the Secretary General (SRSG). They comprised a department with a single, explicit mandate: the protection of children. The department became operational in January 2000 with a team headed by a Child Protection Adviser (CPA), joined later by a Child Protection Officer" (SLTRC 2004a).

Transitional justice initiatives also made provisions for child protection and participation, again, at the urging of the international community. The SLTRC stated in their final report, "In interpreting its mandate the Commission wanted to ensure that the voices of children would be heard and taken into account at every stage of its proceedings, in the various versions of the final report and in the recommendations it made in respect of the future well being of children. The Commission also wanted to ensure that the identity of children who testified would remain confidential. The Commission thus faced a delicate balancing act, which required the development of a number of policies guiding its work."

The Commission drew on previous work by UNICEF to carry out their mandate with respect to children, which said, "The Commission was fortunate enough to have recourse to a report prepared by UNICEF, reflecting the outcomes of a consultative process that UNICEF had organised in 2001 to consider the participation of children in the work of the Commission. The report confirmed the support within the children's sector for children's experiences to be fully accounted for in the work of the Commission. It also highlighted challenges and areas of concern and proposed a variety of measures designed to protect children. The Commission took these proposals into account when designing its operational policies." Not only was the commission interested in the testimony of children, it was also interested in ensuring that children were an integral part of the process:[2]

> The Commission resolved that it would reach out proactively to children so as to ensure their full participation in all aspects of the Commission's work. This approach would include sensitising children as to the role of the TRC, taking statements from them, having them participate in hearings and involving them in special hearings on children. The Commission's main objective in respect of children was to ensure that their voices should be heard, particularly in the final report and recommendations. The Commission also enacted policies to protect the security and well-being of children. The Commission decided as a matter of policy that all children would be treated equally as witnesses whose experiences needed to be captured by the Commission, irrespective of whether they had perpetrated violations. (SLTRC 2004a)

The SCSL[3] also made special provisions for children. Most importantly, perhaps, it was one of the first international tribunals to prosecute people for recruiting child soldiers.[4] The Statute for the Special Court for Sierra Leone (2000), Article 4, states that the court shall have the power to prosecute persons for "conscripting or enlisting children under the age of 15 years into armed forces or groups or using them to participate actively in hostilities."

The SCSL was not only the first case of indictment of child soldier recruiters, but also handed down the first conviction for the crime: "Alex Tamba Brima, Brima Bazzy Kamara and Santigie Borbor Kanu, all senior commanders of the AFRC, were convicted of crimes against humanity and war crimes committed in a non-international armed conflict, including unlawful killings, extermination, rape, acts of terrorism, collective punishment, and mutilation. They were acquitted of sexual slavery and other inhumane acts . . . Remarkably, the decision taken by the Special Court marks the first time in history that individuals have been convicted of war crimes for conscripting and enlisting children under the age of 15 into armed forces or groups and using them to participate actively in hostilities" (Amnesty International 2007).

Innovations in Child Protection: Why Sierra Leone?

All the initiatives I have described so far are innovations in international norms and practices, highlighting to the international community the growing importance of acknowledging the rights and responsibilities of children. Why did so many of these "firsts" happen in Sierra Leone? Almost certainly, the demand for special activities for children did not arise from the populace of Sierra Leone, whose first concern was rebuilding after the war and whose culture is based on respect for elders more than children. Surely, the initial impetus for many of these programs came from international pressure and a deployment of expertise (Geschiere 2003). In the years immediately preceding Lomé, there were important global trends concerning war-affected children. Sierra Leone signed the Convention on the Rights of the Child (CRC) in 1990, as did most other states. In 1996, Graca Machel's landmark report for the UN on the "Impact of Armed Conflict on Children" was published (Machel 1996). Furthermore, child protection had been a part of Demobilization, Disarmament and Reintegration (DDR) activities in Mozambique, and in Liberia before Sierra Leone, and designers of postwar social programming drew on "lessons learned" from those African contexts. Indeed, the issue of child soldiers particularly, and children affected by war more generally, only really came to prominence as an issue in the 1990s (Boyden 1997; Shepler 2005a; Rosen 2005, 2007).

However, it is not that useful to simplify the story into one of pure imposition of Western norms. Certainly, Sierra Leonean adults care deeply about their children, and there is a tradition of care from which to draw. To understand whether the unprecedented concern for "child protection" programming for war-affected children originated from Sierra Leone or from international experts, we must address the question from both the outside in and the inside out. In addition to an understanding of the globalization of Western models of childhood, we must address this question in the context of a nation weakened by a decade of conflict. Often, African governments sign on to conventions due to international pressure without the ability or even the will to enforce them. In Sierra Leone at the time of Lomé, the national child protection mechanisms (namely, the Ministry of Social Welfare, Gender, and Children's Affairs) were so weak that, in some ways, UNICEF and other international actors could set the agenda.

However, I do not see everything that happened in Sierra Leone regarding child protection as a mere imposition. Archibald and Richards (2002, 340) respond to the idea that human rights are "classic 'top-down' instruments of governance and social control" by considering the role of social agency in the making of local cultures of human rights in Sierra Leone. They see the new enthusiasm for rights "not as the embrace of any preexisting global doctrine of rights, but more as an aspect of local social renewal, constrained and shaped by wartime experience" (340). I see Sierra Leoneans using the material and discursive tools of child rights to pursue their own goals, creating new models of childhood at the intersection of the old norms and the newly underwritten Western ideologies of childhood. It is useful to understand the two fields of power as they come together in struggle over social programming. My research on child soldiers describes the ways that young people made strategic use of new child rights discourse. I detailed children learning how to tell the story of their involvement in the conflict via a standard child-soldier narrative (Shepler 2005a, 2005b). This is echoed somewhat by Archibald and Richards (2002), but they see a deeper influence of rights, with youth really rethinking rural gerontocratic politics using the resources of rights. However, it must always be acknowledged that the West is better funded, and therefore donor concerns often drive the debate.[5]

Trends in child protection programming, therefore, have to be seen as the outcome of negotiations between global trends and local realities. What follows is a description of some of the child protection programs in Sierra Leone post-Lomé, described with respect to global trends and local realities.

What Happened on the Ground in Sierra Leone?

What did all of this concern for child protection at the international level look like on the ground in Sierra Leone?

Pre-Lomé Precursors

Of course, there were some child protection activities in Sierra Leone both before and during the war. Long-time UNICEF staffer Andy Brooks reports that, "Although the Lomé Peace Accord is seen as the catalyst to a full-scale DDR programme in Sierra Leone, the framework for such a programme existed prior to Lomé and had been applied in a quite different context" (Brooks 2005, 3). He provides a comprehensive history of events in child protection leading up to Lomé. He notes that

> the Government handed over 370 child soldiers (including 10 girls) from its armed forces on 31 May 1993. The children were absorbed into makeshift demobilisation centres prior to planned family reunification . . . In 1996, The Family Tracing Network, a decentralised system of NGOs in accessible areas of the country was created with a Secretariat in Freetown . . . This network formed the basis of what became the Child Protection Network . . . Between September 1997 and January 1998, 340 child soldiers from the SLA were released and a commitment made to hand over all children under the age of

15 . . . The momentum in dialogue was such that the AFRC had compiled a list of 2000 names for hand over to child protection agencies. It was at this point, in February 1998, that ECOMOG ousted the Junta . . . Prospects for the release of additional children disappeared. (Brooks 2005, 1)

UNICEF was not the only actor involved in pre-Lomé child protection activities. The organization Children Affected by War (CAW), led by Father Momoh, was also very active in the South, and in Freetown, before Lomé. Other agencies, many affiliated with the Catholic Church, were carrying out child protection activities for war-affected children since these activities fit in well with existing programming, such as orphanages and street children's programs. For example, the NGO Family Homes Movement (FHM) grew out of Father Berton's preexisting programs for youth in the East End of Freetown.

Post-Lomé Explosion

It is undeniable that there was an explosion of child protection NGOs in the immediate post-Lomé period. Signboards went up all over the country with the names of new NGOs dedicated to assisting war affected children, probably responding to donor priorities in the United States and Europe. Some of these NGOs were so-called briefcase NGOs—organizations on paper only, produced by a resourceful *savisman* (roughly translated as "hustler" in Krio; Coulter 2004). While I was doing research on reintegration of former child combatants in Sierra Leone from 1999 to 2002, my sense was that new child protection organizations were forming every day. At the Child Protection Committee meetings in Freetown every month, fledgling child protection groups were in attendance at almost every gathering. Exact numbers are hard to come by since some of these NGOs likely did not even register with the government, and government agencies were not keeping very good records at the time. Recent efforts to determine the year-by-year figures on number of registered child protection NGOs in the country from the MSWGCA[6] and from SLANGO (the Sierra Leone Association of NGOs) yielded unsatisfying results. Just to give a sense of the range of child protection NGOs that sprouted up at that time, those registered with the ministry in 1999 but no longer existing today include Tomsonia Children's Center, Mission East Trust Orphanage, Reach the Kids, Yamakai Orphanage, Mother Care Orphanage, and The Association for the Care and Up-Bringing of Children and Young Persons. In contrast, most of the international child protection agencies in operation in 1999 are still operating today. The real decline is in the number of small local child protection NGOs. The number of beneficiaries per agency is generally small (from the tens up to a hundred), and ten years after the war, they are working with "vulnerable children," "orphans," and "street children," whereas in the past, the target population would have been "war-affected children."

Reintegration of Former Child Soldiers

Reintegration of former child soldiers, or Demobilization, Disarmament, and Reintegration (DDR) for Children Affiliated with Fighting Factions (CAFF), in the agency parlance, is the most well-known type of postwar programming for children. Under the umbrella of UNICEF, several international agencies took on the task. The TRC, drawing on data from the National Commission on DDR (NCDDR), reports that in total, 6,774 children were put through the DDR process. Of this number, 6,261 were male and 513 were female. Along factional lines, the division was as follows: 3,710 RUF; 2,026 CDF; 471 SLA; 427 AFRC; 84 from other factions; and 60 nonaffiliated child combatants (TRC).[7] Child protection agencies performed a number of different activities in support of DDR for CAFF. They set up Interim Care Centres (ICCs) for immediate reception of demobilized children. These centers provided medical treatment as well as psychosocial programming. They performed family tracing and reunification as well as community sensitization. As I said above, some of this work was started before Lomé, but, in general, the smaller more local agencies (such as Christian Brothers) gave way to bigger international agencies (such as the International Rescue Committee; IRC) as the postwar period progressed. At the height of DDR activities, the main players were IRC, Caritas Makeni, and Cooperation Internazionale (COOPI).

According to present day UNICEF reports,

> UNICEF's Child Protection programme provides co-ordination, strategic direction and financial support to actors working to protect children and their rights. This includes initiatives to ensure that children are provided with the appropriate care and protection through disarmament, demobilisation, emergency care and reunification processes. Since the end of the disarmament, demobilization and reunification (DDR), there has been no child abduction by armed forces. Many of the children who were registered as "separated" within the DDR Programme have been reunited with their families. Consequently, all but three of the interim care centres have closed and the family tracing and reunification scaled down. These have been replaced by a system of community-based reintegration programmes, whereby every reunified child will be supported in their home environment that includes work with the other children in the home community. (United Nations Children's Fund Sierra Leone 2004)

On my visits to Sierra Leone in 2007 and 2009, there were very few programs still in operation for CAFF. I found that all the programs for former child soldiers I had known in 2000 were shut down, and other programs I had read about and hoped to visit were not really operating. The Sierra Leone Government report to the UN Committee on the Rights of the Child notes that Sierra Leone has achieved successes with regards to child soldiers. UNICEF's 2004 country program document also reports success with the child soldier issue, "Since the end of the disarmament and demobilization in January 2002, there has been no abduction of children by armed forces." They further report that 98 percent of children who were registered as separated have been reunified with their families and center-based care has been replaced by community-based support (UNICEF 2004). Perhaps more importantly, a 2006 study carried out by Search for Common Ground to evaluate their partnership with NGOs and community organizations to implement UNICEF's national Child Protection campaign reported that, overall, reintegration was not viewed as a priority (Search for Common Ground 2006). Indeed, the Sierra Leonean respondents seemed much more concerned about child exploitation and abuse than the direct effects of the war. This is an interesting outcome, given that ten years ago, it was assumed internationally that a "lost generation" of former child combatants would be a lasting impact of the war.

Non-DDR Activities

Of course, in addition to the ICCs, there were many other child-protection activities going on in Sierra Leone during the postwar period. For example, the Ministry of Education, together with UNICEF, developed programs for accelerated schooling for children whose education had been disrupted by the war. Schools were set up in IDP and refugee camps. There were special programs for child amputees and girls who had been abducted as "bush wives" (Coulter 2005). As above, many of these programming initiatives originated with international concerns. Indeed, one can almost always observe a close connection between trends at the international level and programs at the local level.

In particular, after about 2002, there was an upsurge in the number of programs for girls. I believe this increase was largely a result of reports such as "Where are the Girls? Girls in Fighting Forces in Northern Uganda, Sierra Leone and Mozambique: Their Lives During and After War" (McKay and Mazurana 2004). Of course, groups such as Forum for African Women Educationalists (FAWE) existed before the trend, and were well positioned to take advantage of it and build on their preexisting work on girls' education. Other trends included bumps in programs for youth livelihoods in response to UNDP, and other reports about the effect of "youth bulges" on the onset of conflict and the need to deflect dissatisfied youth from rebellion (UNDP 2006; Urdal 2004). When UNICEF and others took up the fight against child trafficking in the mid-2000s, there was a shift away from orphanages due to the fear that transnational adoptions could be perceived as human trafficking. Now the Sierra Leone Government proudly reports that it is literally impossible for any foreigner to adopt a child from Sierra Leone.

There is also what we might call niche programming in child protection. Defense of Children International–Sierra Leone has long been involved in juvenile justice issues, including monitoring the remand home. Talking Drum Studio, a radio production organization and the Sierra Leone branch of the international NGO Search for Common Ground, produces programs on youth political participation, as well as the *Golden Kids News*, a news show by and for children. Different perspectives on youth, whether they are viewed as potentially dangerous or potentially victims, yield different types of programming.[8]

Alongside the local-level programming in response to global trends in protection, there is the ongoing project of monitoring and reporting to international bodies. Some of the organizations participating in this project are the Coalition to Stop the Use of Child Soldiers, the Special Representative of the Secretary General on Children in Armed Conflict, and the UN Office of the High Commissioner for Human Rights Committee on the Rights of the Child.

Finally, the biggest news in child protection in Sierra Leone is the passage of the National Child Rights Bill in June 2007. UNICEF in Sierra Leone reports that the bill "represents a unique opportunity for making a number of national laws and policies more aligned with international standards, which is unprecedented in the history of Sierra Leone" (UNICEF 2007). The government of Sierra Leone reported to the UN that "there was no discrimination by law, but through cultural beliefs and practices" (UNICEF 2007). However, Search for Common Ground reports that among Sierra Leoneans they surveyed, there was little focus on the Child Rights Bill since "it conflicts with traditional views of caregiving and is difficult for many to understand." (Search for Common Ground 2006, 2). So if the "cultural beliefs and practices" of the people are in the way of child protection, in a sense, we have come around again to the question of whether child protection innovations in Sierra Leone come from the outside or the inside. Again, is the Child Rights Bill a representation of Sierra Leoneans' own concerns with the status of children in their country, or is it an imposition of Western standards?

Political Ramifications for Youth

Noting the disjuncture between the aspirations of international treaties on children's rights and the reality of children's lives in Africa, Rwezaura (1998, 253) argues that "any effort to raise the status of an African child must begin with an appreciation of the current social and economic context given that it is such a powerful force on the lives of most children in Sub-Saharan Africa." So apart from programming and changes in the law, for a moment, let us begin with the "current social and economic context" for children in Sierra Leone.

In what ways has childhood and youth changed in Sierra Leone since Lomé? In many ways the life of the average child in Sierra Leone is not too different than before the war. Education and health data are still abysmal. The Search for Common Ground evaluation cited previously reports that there is a great deal of knowledge concerning child rights, though there is still resistance to change. To me, the really fascinating developments for youth are not those coming from International NGO-sponsored programs. Krijn Peters (2007) has written about the phenomenon of motorcycle taxi (*okada*) drivers in Sierra Leone, and the way these young men, many of them ex-combatants, have organized themselves across fighting factions in postwar Sierra Leone. I have recently written about the phenomenon of young people's interventions in the political sphere through an explosion of pop music about corruption and the political position of youth (Shepler 2008). In my opinion, these refashionings of child and youth identity that grow out of the social and political context are far more vital than child rights sensitization that seeks to impose a notion of proper childhood from afar and, even with the best intentions, render children and youth apolitical.[9]

Conclusion

Sierra Leone is now "post-post-conflict" (Errante 2000), the big donors are gone, and the child protection agenda looks very different than it did immediately after Lomé. UNICEF is still doing its traditional work in child protection: health, nutrition, and education. The local NGOs have reduced in number as the funds for war-affected youth have dried up. Richards (1996) famously said that grievances around education, unemployment, and political representation of youth are key to understanding the causes of the war. To what extent have child protection activities in Sierra Leone addressed the issues of the so-called crisis of youth? Those issues go beyond child protection and go right to the heart of the grievances underlying the conflict. For now, the focus seems to be on reacting to internationally defined concerns more than on the potentially revolutionary act of responding to, or even fostering, local constituencies for children and youth.

Notes

1. I use "regime" in Foucault's sense, as a meeting of power, knowledge, and practice.
2. Another innovation was the creation of a child's version of the TRC report: "The child-friendly version of our Truth and Reconciliation Commission Report for Sierra Leone is unprecedented. No truth commission in the past has produced such a report. This report is ground breaking in other respects, including the participation of representatives of children's groups in its content, language, and design. The Commission hopes that it will be widely distributed, both in Sierra Leone and in other countries" (SLTRC 2004b, 5).
3. The SCSL was a hybrid court combining international tribunal and national law. In particular, the Statute for the Special Court's Article 5 notes the following offenses under existing Sierra Leonean law: "a. Offences relating to the abuse of girls under the Prevention of Cruelty to Children Act, 1926 (Cap. 31): i. Abusing a girl under 13 years of age, contrary to section 6; ii. Abusing a girl between 13 and 14 years of age, contrary to section 7; iii. Abduction of a girl for immoral purposes, contrary to section 12." Finally, provisions were put in place to modernize Sierra Leonean justice systems to bring them into line with existing international standards. Article 7 states that "the Special Court shall have no jurisdiction over any person who was under the age of 15 at the time of the alleged commission of the crime. Should any person who was at the time of the alleged commission of the crime between 15 and 18 years of age come before the Court, he or she shall be treated with dignity and a sense of worth, taking into account his or her young age and the desirability of promoting his or her rehabilitation, reintegration into and assumption of a constructive role in society, and in accordance with international human rights standards, in particular the rights of the child." See Sanin and Sirnemann (2006) for an in-depth study of the participation of children at the SCSL.
4. The Rome Statute of the International Criminal Court took on the task, and has since indicted several people from the Democratic Republic of Congo for recruitment of children into armed forces.
5. A very clear example of this struggle can be found in the recent (May 2008) report of government of Sierra Leone to the UN Commission on the Rights of the Child. There is a very interesting back-and-forth between the UN committee and Teresa Vamoi, Chief Social Development Officer and the head of the Sierra Leone delegation.
6. Thanks to Gibrila Fofanah for research assistance in Freetown, trying to gather comprehensive data from the ministry there.

7. As Andy Brooks notes, there were different numbers reported for separated children by the MSWGCA, who had their own registration system. They registered 2,811 as abducted by the RUF and 516 as enlisting with the fighting forces. Overall, record keeping and data tracking were poor throughout the exercise.

8. Yvonne Kemper (2005) does a nice job of detailing the various types of programming for children and youth associated with various perspectives on youth and conflict.

9. See the recent thesis by Sabrina Karim (2008) on the limitations inherent in NGO programs that encourage youth participation while based on a framework containing disempowering assumptions about childhood.

References

Amnesty International. 2007. Sierra Leone: Guilty verdicts not the end of the story for victims of war crimes. Press release, June 21. http://www.amnesty.org/en/library/info/AFR51/003/2007.

Archibald, Steven, and Paul Richards. 2002. Converts to human rights? Popular debate about war and justice in rural central Sierra Leone. *Africa* 72 (3): 339–67.

Boyden, Jo. 1997. Childhood and the policy makers: A comparative perspective on the globalization of childhood. In *Constructing and reconstructing childhood: Contemporary issues in the sociological study of childhood*, ed. Allison James and Alan Prout, 190–229. London: Falmer Press.

Brooks, Andrew. 2005. *The disarmament, demobilisation, and reintegration of children associated with the fighting forces: Lessons learned in Sierra Leone 1998–2002.* Dakar, Senegal: Imprimerie Graphi Plus.

Coulter, Chris. 2004. "The aid business is my business": Young men and the humanitarian regime in post-war Sierra Leone. Unpublished manuscript. Department of Anthropology, Uppsala University, Sweden.

———. 2005. Assessment of the "Girls Left Behind" project for girls and young women who did not go through the DDR process in Sierra Leone. Evaluation sponsored by UNICEF. Freetown: UNICEF.

Errante, Antionette. 2000. Child soldiers as casualties of the post-conflict policy environment: When is a country post-post-war? Paper presented at conference, Children and Armed Conflict: Reintegration of Former Child Soldiers in the Post-Conflict Community, Tokyo, Japan.

Geschiere, Peter. 2003. On witch doctors and spin doctors: The role of "experts" in African and American politics. In *Magic and modernity: Interfaces of revelation and concealment*, ed. Birgit Meyer and Peter Pels, 159–82. Stanford: Stanford University Press.

Karim, Sabrina. 2008. Humanitarianism and the role of young people in conflict: Challenges to the current normative framework of children's participation. MA thesis, Oxford University.

Kemper, Yvonne. 2005. *Youth in war-to-peace transitions: Approaches of international organizations.* Berlin: Berghof Research Center for Constructive Conflict Management.

Lomé Peace Accord. 1999. Peace agreement between the government of Sierra Leone and the Revolutionary United Front of Sierra Leone. http://www.sierra-leone.org/lomeaccord.html.

Machel, Graça. 1996. *Impact of armed conflict on children.* New York: United Nations.

McKay, Susan, and Dyan Mazurana. 2004. *Where are the girls? Girls in fighting forces in Northern Uganda, Sierra Leone and Mozambique: Their lives during and after war.* Montreal: CIDA, Rights and Democracy.

Peters, Krijn. 2007. From weapons to wheels: Young Sierra Leonean ex-combatants become motorbike taxi-riders. *Peace, Conflict & Development* 10:1–23.

Richards, Paul. 1996. *Fighting for the rain forest: War, youth & resources in Sierra Leone.* Oxford: James Currey.

Rosen, David. 2005. *Armies of the young: Child soldiers in war and terrorism.* New Brunswick, NJ: Rutgers University Press.

———. 2007. Child soldiers, international humanitarian law, and the globalization of childhood. *American Anthropologist* 109 (2): 296–306.

Rwezaura, Bart. 1998. Competing "images" of childhood in the social and legal systems of contemporary sub-Saharan Africa. *International Journal of Law, Policy and the Family* 12 (3): 253–78.

Sanin, Kyra, and Anna Stirnemann. 2006. *Child witnesses at the special court for Sierra Leone.* Berkeley: War Crimes Studies Center, University of California.

Search for Common Ground. 2006. Key findings from the National Child Protection Campaign: A report on the intervention of Search for Common Ground. http://www.sfcg.org/Programmes/sierra/programmes_sierra.html#5b.

Shepler, Susan. 2005a. *Conflicted childhoods: Fighting over child soldiers in Sierra Leone.* PhD diss., University of California, Berkeley.

———. 2005b. The rites of the child: Global discourses of youth and reintegrating child soldiers in Sierra Leone. *Journal of Human Rights* 4 (2): 197–212.

———. 2008. "Now di Pa de Pak foh Go": Young Sierra Leoneans' musical interventions in post-war politics. Paper presented at *Shake, Rattle: Music, Conflict, and Change.* Experience Music Project, Seattle.

Sierra Leone Truth and Reconciliation Commission. 2004a. *The final report of the Truth and Reconciliation Commission of Sierra Leone,* vol. 3b. Ghanian Community of Greater Lowell, Ghana: Graphic Packaging, Ltd. http://www.sierra-leone.org/Other-Conflict/TRCVolume3B.pdf.

Sierra Leone Truth and Reconciliation Commission. 2004b. Truth and reconciliation report for the children of Sierra Leone. http://www.unicef.org/infobycountry/files/TRCCF9SeptFINAL.pdf.

United Nations Children's Fund. 2007. Sierra Leone Approves the National Child Rights Bill. Press release, June 7. http://www.unicef.org/media/media_39951.html.

United Nations Children's Fund Sierra Leone. 2004. Revised country programme document: Sierra Leone. Report to United Nations Children's Fund executive

board, presented at the first regular session, January 19–23 and 26. http://www
.unicef.org/about/execboard/files/Sierra-Leone-CPD-rev.pdf.

United Nations Development Programme. 2006. *Youth and violent conflict: Society
and development in crisis?* New York: UNDP.

United Nations and the Government of Sierra Leone. 2000. *Statute of the special
court for Sierra Leone.* Established by an agreement between the United Nations
and the government of Sierra Leone pursuant to security council resolution
1315, August 14.

Urdal, Henrik. 2004. *The devil in the demographics: The effect of youth bulges on
domestic armed conflict, 1950–2000.* Washington, DC: The World Bank.

Part II

Beyond Lomé

5

Article 27

Citizens, Refugees, and Relief along the Sierra Leone-Guinea Border

M. Douglas Henry

You know, the Guineans here used to tell us that before refugees came into this area, they didn't even know that this was part of Guinea. There was *nothing* here—no roads, only bushpaths. But after we'd been here about 3 months, a UN worker visited us, and told us to come down from there, that all refugees should be in a camp . . . But a lot of people wanted to stay in town, they didn't want to come down. But the UN said, "No, we won't allow refugees to stay there; refugees should be in the camp. If you're in the town, then we won't regard you as a refugee. And we won't carry supplies up to you in the town."

—Kolomba Camp Secretary, narrating a history
of Kolomba Refugee Camp, Guinea

Article 27 of the Lomé accord allows for the provision of humanitarian relief in the country, in that the signing parties agree to the safe and unhindered access by all humanitarian organizations throughout the country. The government additionally promises to set up effective administrative or security bodies capable of monitoring and facilitating the implementation of these guarantees within the areas in which humanitarian organizations operate. Though relief aid had supported Internally Displaced Persons (IDPs) and refugees on either side of the border from

---

This article is based on thirteen months of medical anthropology fieldwork, living in two camps for displaced persons on either side of the Sierra Leone-Guinea border.

shortly after the outbreak of the war, the Lomé Peace Accord signaled a process whereby massive networks of relief providers were granted access to areas hitherto largely not accessed or ignored on the part of formalized state governance. This chapter discusses the impact of Article 27, and the relief processes it represents, on shaping the consciousness of national identity.

It is important to note that the Sierra Leone conflict entered the country in the distant margins of the Sierra Leonean and Guinean states by borders initially far from both Freetown and Conakry's reach. In these frontier areas, ethnically Mende and Kissi inhabitants could freely cross back and forth across the Meli River between Sierra Leone and Guinea to trade, hunt, or visit family. This changed dramatically with the 1991 conflict, in which at least 2 million people became displaced either internally within the country or across the border into Guinea or Liberia. In Sierra Leone, infrastructural damage has been enormous—schools, banks, health clinics, bridges, churches, and hospitals were damaged or destroyed; many are still beyond repair years after the Lomé accord.

The significance of the violence has been variously interpreted as a mixture of personal political grievances harbored by neighboring Liberia's President Charles Taylor (widely acknowledged to support the rebels), war-inspired exiles and youth radicals fighting social exclusion and failed patrimonialism, and increased criminal control over the highly profitable illicit diamond trade. Yet for the ethnically Mende and Kissi peoples on either side of the Meli River, the war had very different meanings and different significances. At the local level, the inhabitants of the region experienced not only the influx of tens of thousands of strangers, but also the massive mobilization of the international system of humanitarian relief, as dozens of humanitarian agencies, and hundreds of Western employees and consultants representing the relief community, entered the region to provide assistance. Within the span of several months, areas that had never been visited by a high-ranking government official were seeing soldiers, roads, Land Cruisers, wells, schools, health clinics, and teams of Europeans. As the camp secretary pointed out to me in the opening story, for the many people at the margins who "didn't know this was part of Guinea," the influx meant a "discovery" of the border for many, and a sudden affirmation, if not awareness, of identity, citizenship, and national belonging. For the people living at the margins, suddenly divided into categories of "refugees" and "citizens," this awareness was experienced as ambivalent at best. For both refugees and citizens alike, learning to adapt to the system providing aid was at least as important as learning to adapting to the presence of each other.

Relief at the Margins

Scholars have noted how the relative vacuum left by the formal contraction of the postcolonial African state can produce dispersed agents of power, as warlords or regional strongmen may rebel in an attempt to recover or maintain control of dwindling state resources (Mbembe 1992; Ayoob 1995; Reno 1998). Centralized governments may subvert would-be challengers by turning to either commercially contracted military forces or multilateral alliances (United Nations [UN] peacekeepers, international aid agencies) to assume duties and responsibilities formerly performed by centralized governments. These arrangements are often mutually beneficial. Government leaders may prefer them as a way of maintaining their control, in that they cede some of the responsibilities of the formal state, and allow the development of a "shadow state" more adept at resource procurement and personal profit (Reno 1992). Refugee relief and management agencies such as the office for the United Nations High Commissioner for Refugees (UNHCR) may prefer the smoother operations that exist under a stable, central authority rather than having to deal with the chaos afforded by a myriad of local forces. Foreign aid agencies and international nongovernmental organizations (NGOs), for example, may free up limited state resources and ease state responsibility in that the relief regime can take over the functions of social services like education, health care, welfare, or economic stimulation for large groups of people (Harrell Bond 1986; Marchal 1987; Mazur 1988).

The history of the modern system of international humanitarian relief has received recent attention from scholars (Gallagher 1989; Malkki 1995), as has the ambivalent nature of its entry into countries in conflict. Critics note the singular tendency of the "refugee regime" to act as a "global state," implementing top-down models which preclude situational flexibility or genuine local participation (Harrell Bond 1993; Zolberg, Suhrke, and Aguayo 1989; de Waal 1997), or for functionalist and "sedentarist" biases that pathologize refugees, encouraging aggressive, external interventions, or for the "restricting logic" that refugee camp policies impose on their inhabitants, creating dependent, helpless, powerless populations (Malkki 1992; Roe 1995; Kleinman and Kleinman 1997). Malkki, for example, notes that humanitarian knowledge is discursively powerful, and may operate to silence refugee agendas that run contrary to its own (Malkki 1996). Operating as a neocolonial managerial force, relief regimes may negate local knowledge in their efforts to produce a "speechlessness" that "blocks the possibilities of persons stepping forward from the milling crowds, asking for the microphone, and addressing the glassy eye of the camera" (Malkki 1996: 390). All of these tendencies could be seen operating in varying

degrees in the treatment of displacement along the Sierra Leone-Guinea border. However, over time, local people learned adaptive strategies to deploy
their own manipulations, ways to counter foreign attempts at control or definition, and ways to subvert the silencing strategies of their external management—ways of effectively standing up to the microphone and demanding
dialogue on the world stage.

The Mission to Divide and Contain

As in much of Africa, the forested border areas between Sierra Leone and
Guinea cut across ethnic groups. At least before 1991, population mobility
across the border was high, as people migrated between towns and farms for
family responsibilities, educational opportunities, or employment strategies.
This meant that in Guinea, some of the people displaced from Sierra Leone
arrived in areas inhabited by their own extended families. During the initial
influx, they became absorbed into relationships defined by preexisting social
structures such as family, "strangers," or "hosts." One Guinean elder characterized the arrival of people into his village in this way: "Before the war, we
used to come and go on both sides, so there had been a lot of mixing among
us. So such a person, when you meet trouble, you must go to your brother.
We're all the same. When they cry, we cry" (Aruna, Luankoli village, Guinea).

This preexisting sameness, however, was not immediately recognized by
the UNHCR, for whom the crossing of a state boundary meant a dissection
of identities, as people became split into categories of "refugees" and "citizens." This distinction became extremely important locally, as the UNHCR's
definitions were not identified as merely technical, neutral record-taking,
but as politically infused acts with the potential to include or exclude people
from assistance that could benefit their lives, for which side of the border
one was identified with was crucial in determining the quality and quantity
of foreign relief provisions. Refugees got supply items like food, tarpaulins,
buckets, mats, and pots; at least initially, citizens could only look on envi-
ously. This was unfortunate, considering that the conditions of citizens were
often just as bad as that for refugees. Jealousy and conflict could easily result,
because the UN's actions could mean that the quality of life of the "poor"
refugees the citizens had been hosting could suddenly improve beyond their
own. One Guinean man told me indignantly,

> It's not only the refugees that suffer inside of this war. We, during the time
> when they came into our village, it was so difficult to get food. There was
> no room in the village to move around, and the bush surrounding the vil-
> lage quickly became used up. I was the "Secretary" here at the time. We all

wrote our names down (on the UNHCR refugee registration lists), but got nothing. We tried to register in Kondou, and then in Kolomba town, but no way . . . not even 1 kg. of supply. Some of our refugees got supplies, but the citizens, who were feeding them and supporting them, we got nothing. When the supplies came, they said our names were not "inside." Even now our swamps, our plantations, and our farms are exhausted. (Mamadii, Luankoli village, Guinea.)

UNHCR acted to separate citizens from refugees in both abstract and physical space. Citing concerns of cholera, refugees were told to move out of the hilltop Guinean village of Kolomba, and to build rows of "baffas" (huts) in the fields below. When asked why this was so, the Kolomba camp secretary answered: "I guess they don't want you to mix yourself with the citizens. Because the food they were bringing was just for refugees, and *the citizens were just the ones serving it* in the camp. And only the ones in the camp could register (Kolomba camp secretary; emphasis mine). The secretary's perspective that the citizens were just there to "serve" the relief provisions indicates just how far the UNHCR's separations changed the local perspective on the proper roles of "citizens" and "refugees." They undermined what had been mutually supportive relationships and increased the conflictual space between the two created categories of people. The result was actually negative for both groups, in that it threatened both the well being of the Guinean hosts and the security of refugees; the envy of citizens could turn to actual violence.[1] Whereas the distribution of food and the sharing of commodities used to come under long-standing cultural obligations of either interdependent family or hosts and strangers, the UN's view was that these people, their vulnerabilities, and their sources of food were distinct. This perspective was often at odds with the real situation at hand.[2]

Amitav Ghosh provides a useful analytical lens on this situation through his analysis of UN peacekeeping forces as active agents in defining the boundaries of the non-Western world. Ghosh (1994) notes an inherent logic to the UN's actions, as it represents the total of the world's recognized nation-states—"the logic of its functioning is to recreate its membership wherever it goes." Humanitarianism becomes an instrument and an exercise in restoring and recreating the nation-state. The irony (especially given the quote by Aruna) is that agents or agencies from Western countries become empowered to cross borders (e.g., *médecins sans frontières*), while the local people from non-Western countries are confronted with a border that is increasingly closed. Ghosh concludes that it is extremely ironic that the UN, embraced by third world people as a symbol of opportunity and freedom, becomes an instrument of their containment.

For Guinean citizens living in the marginalized border areas, the violence, in effect, provided a structuring idiom that allowed them to apprehend the crisis of their own state marginality. The fact that their "new" label of "citizen" now excluded them from international relief supplies came as a painful shock; especially when most had never perceived any benefits of "citizenship" in the first place. The international rush to provide relief to refugees revealed what they, as citizens, had always lacked, such as proper wells, supported schools, and well-stocked clinics.

"Stepping Up" to the Microphone

Significantly, however, though they may have suffered initial indignity at their apprehended marginality, citizens quickly learned to manipulate the system so as to receive what they saw as their "rightful" share. They learned they could counter the UN's definitions by situationally reconfiguring their own presented identities to "become" refugees. During fieldwork, in a camp about a half-hour's walk from Kolomba, a new dwelling appeared just inside the camp across from the central well. It was constructed out of concrete, with a nice cement verandah and a metal roof (this was odd because most houses were waddle-and-daub with thatched roofs covered by the omnipresent UNHCR tarpaulins). A guide explained quietly, "That 'refugee's' old house in the village was too far from the well." The house, in fact, belonged to a citizen-"turned"-refugee.

By moving themselves into the camps, Guineans were not only moving closer to the "state" services they had been missing, they were, in effect, choosing a "refugee identity" by negotiating the relief supply system and manipulating the system into giving them supplies.[3] In that this identity could be invoked situationally (depending on the potential to receive relief aid), it was less hard and fast than the UN's, and more in line with the ambiguity that had existed before the war, as when people had moved freely from one side of the border to another. Aruna, a Kissi man I met in a Guinean village near Kolomba, explained to me the practicality guiding many citizens' decisions: "In fact, when people first came, we all built *baffas* (in Kolomba Camp). So in case of anything like supply came, we would have those places there for us. And we usually try to keep one of our brothers there, so that if . . . he hears of anything going on, we still have someplace to go . . . Some supplies they only supply you if you have a baffa, so it's better to leave someone there."

To be fair, the UN became aware of the disparities and ill relations their definitions could create between well-supplied refugees and their poorer hosts, and took actions to prevent it. Later programs, though often instigated through international NGOs several months or years after the initial influx, included special "development" supplies of seeds, food, and agricultural tools for Guineans. Health services for refugees in Guinea were somewhat an exception to this, in that they were actually operated by the Guinean Ministry of Health—under the *Programme d'Assistance aux Réfugiés Libériens et Sierra-léonais* (PARLS)—and, in theory, delivered services for refugees and citizens alike. This system was created to grant refugees free access to preexisting Guinean health facilities, and, simultaneously, to reinforce local health centers and district hospitals to enable them to handle the additional strain (Van Damme 1998). In many cases, however, the preexisting services were in such a state of disrepair that new facilities had to be constructed, almost always located near the center of the camps.

Guineans were not alone in their manipulation of identities; at times, it was useful for refugees to represent themselves to the relief system as citizens. In 1997, for example, one American NGO had decided to encourage people to form local "work cooperatives" by supplying farming tools, seed rice, and "food-for-work." Cooperatives were to make more efficient use of land surrounding the camps for farming. They were supposedly culturally appropriate based on existing African styles of sharing work; they were models for refugee self-help, believed capable of steering refugees away from undesirable "dependency" by encouraging them toward self-sufficiency. Work cooperatives were open to both refugees and citizens; agency representatives professed a belief that the cooperatives would foster a sense of mutual cooperation and good will between the two groups.

In part because they were accountable to international donors for supplies handed out, relief agencies on the ground felt the need to demonstrate responsibility by counting, and closely monitoring, recipients. This could easily run afoul of refugees themselves, who prioritized the need to mask or overreport their numbers in order to gain increased relief entitlements. Refugee names listed in the cooperatives were subject to "verification checks"—comparing registered project names to official preregistered refugee names on file with UNHCR in the regional town of Guéckédou—in an effort to ensure that no one would "cheat" the system by multiply-listing their names. Guineans, whose names were not on any such refugee list, were exempt from such verification. A second method was supposed to verify Guineans—this was to "spot-check," or randomly show up at a cooperative farm site, asking to see the workers listed on a project registration card. This required the cooperative members to sit at the farm site, often for hours, waiting for the arrival of the verification team, or to anticipate, ahead of time, what farm sites might be visited, and hastily do some work to make the area appear to be "actively" farmed. At times, agency representatives would ask the children present what the names of their parents were, to see if the child's response matched up with the names recorded on the cards. Even though children were coached, there could be tremendous pressure and tension inherent in this interaction, as the relief supplies directly affected a family's subsistence.

These cooperatives, though well intentioned, were somewhat unrealistic, as envisioned by the NGO. In truth, there is some local basis for "traditional" work cooperatives. For the Mende of this region, a *clohbi* (or it is occasionally named *kombi*) does exist as a mutual support mechanism whereby farmers can recruit laborers and provide mutual support around farm preparation or harvest. The NGO cooperatives, however, bore little resemblance to these, and were not identified by refugees as being similar. Whereas a *clohbi* was typically small and governed by kinship or society ties, work cooperatives were large, depersonalized entities. While a *clohbi* was typically organized around a specific need such as home building or harvesting, cooperative projects were not so much self-initiated as imposed, through the promise of food-for-work for farming around the camp.

Because they bore little resemblance to preexisting work groups, refugees saw no need to apply customary rules or ethics to their organization. Instead, they quickly learned to exploit the new system. The primary method was to invent extra citizen involvement in the project, as projects with more members received more food aid. In many cases, a single refugee could assume dual or multiple citizen identities to a visiting verification team, often across several projects, presenting as both refugee and citizen applicant. Through manipulating their numbers to be higher, refugees were able to make their situation appear more vulnerable, thereby both procuring more supply and continuing to draw international support for their situation. In reality, perhaps, they were so successful partly because the priority of high numbers was shared by both relief agencies and the displaced. Both shared an interest in reporting and recording high numbers—refugees in order to gain more entitlements, and agencies in order to procure more international donations and extend their international mandate for local work.

Conclusions

By bringing light to these local manipulations, particularly in the face of the high-minded language and ideals of the Lomé accord, or the genuine concern that often pervades humanitarian organizations, one runs the risk of glibly portraying Sierra Leoneans and Guineans living along the border as "unneedy" or perhaps ungrateful, fraudulent "schemers." This would be a tremendous disservice. The people living in and around the camps where I myself lived and researched were often sick, malnourished, hungry, disempowered, and poor. Few local citizens, and almost no refugees, grew rich. Their actions do, however, illustrate how identity along the margins of the state can resist external definition, whether imposed upon it by the state or by state-like agents, in this case, international agencies providing humanitarian relief. The people at the margins learned to subvert these attempts at dissection by negotiating and manipulating the system that produced them. Identities became more situational, flexible, and ambiguous, negotiated in ways that were locally beneficial. Refugees could become citizens; citizens could become refugees.

This negotiation had further significance. People discovered that there was power in manipulating identity, in that assumed status or postured numbers communicated vulnerability in a loud voice (literally heard around the world) and ensured continued aid arriving in the camp from abroad. The people on the margins had discovered, in effect, a way of "standing up to the microphone" of communicating distress on the international stage. Of course, all of this maneuvering was not without problem, and analysis should be cautious of overly romanticizing resistant actors. Power exerted by relief agencies is very effective, and quite often silences alternative possibilities. Ironically, manipulations of vulnerability by refugees, intended to keep global attention focused on their plight, often reinforced "helpless" stereotypes that seemed to justify continued aggressive external intervention and management. Again, however, most people living around the border areas wanted this, as it signaled what they saw as the real role of international donors, which was to bring relief supplies or state services into the marginal areas so that they could buy, sell, or manage them in order to make a better life. In the processes institutionalized by Article 27, identity became a central issue in an unfolding dialogue between donors and recipients, a dialogue about personal agency and "vulnerability," where meanings like "citizen" and "refugee" became renegotiated and reconfigured, and where creative coping strategies and local resistance began.

Notes

1. I heard countless stories of vengeful citizens setting fire to a refugee baffa, or spreading rumors of a particular refugee–rebel collaboration in order to draw Guinean soldiers into driving the refugee away from the camp.
2. Melissa Leach offers a similar view into how relief aid upset the previously existing patron–client relationships among Liberian refugees and their Mende hosts in Sierra Leone (Leach 1992).

3. In a similar vein, Ferme (1998) notes that, at least since the time of the "hut tax," census taking and numbering people in Sierra Leone has never been a neutral activity, but has become associated with "control" or "exposure." At one time, underrepresenting one's numbers was important, as counting could be linked to taxation, labor conscription, or an undesirable incorporation into the state; at other times, over-representing could be good, in order to obtain development benefits

References

Ayoob, Mohammed. 1995. *The third world security predicament: State making, regional conflict, and the international system.* Boulder, CO: Lynne Rienner.

de Waal, Alex. 1997. *Famine crimes: Politics and the disaster relief industry in Africa.* Oxford: African Rights and James Currey.

Ferme, Mariane. 1998. The violence of numbers: Consensus, competition, and the negotiation of disputes in Sierra Leone. *Cahiers d'études africaines* 38 (150–52): 555–80.

Gallagher, Dennis. 1989. The evolution of the international refugee system. *International Migration Review* 23:579–98.

Ghosh, Amitav. 1994. The global reservation: Notes toward an ethnography of international peacekeeping. *Cultural Anthropology* 9 (3): 412–22.

Harrell-Bond, Barbara. 1986. *Imposing aid: Emergency assistance to refugees.* Oxford: Oxford University Press.

———. 1993. Creating marginalised dependent minorities: Relief programs for refugees in Europe. *Refugee Studies Program Newsletter* 15:14–17.

Kleinman, Arthur, and Joan Kleinman. 1997. The appeal of experience; the dismay of images: Cultural appropriations of suffering in out times. In *Social suffering,* ed. Arthur Kleinman, Veena Das, and Margaret Lock, 1–24. Berkeley: University of California Press.

Leach, Melissa. 1992. *Dealing with displacement. IDS Research Reports 22.* Sussex: Institute of Development Studies.

Malkki, Liisa. 1992. National Geographic: The rooting of peoples and the territorialization of national identity among scholars and refugees. *Cultural Anthropology* 7 (1): 24–44.

———. 1995. Refugees and exile: From "refugee studies" to the national order of things. *Annual Review of Anthropology* 24:495–523.

———. 1996. Speechless emissaries: Refugees, humanitarianism, and dehistoricization. *Cultural Anthropology* 11 (3): 377–404.

Marchal, Roland. 1987. Production sociale et recomposition dans l'éxile: le cas Érythréen. *Cahiers d'études africaines* 27 (3–4): 393–410.

Mazur, Robert. 1988. Refugees in Africa: The role of sociological analysis and praxis. *Current Sociology* 36:43–60.

Mbembe, Achille. 1992. Provisional notes on the postcolony. *Africa* 62 (1): 3–37.

Reno, Will. 1992. *Corruption and state politics in Sierra Leone.* Cambridge: Cambridge University Press.

———. 1998. *Warlord politics and African states*. Boulder, CO: Lynne Rienner.

Roe, Emery. 1995. Except Africa: postscript to a special section on development narratives. *World Development* 23 (6): 1065–69.

Van Damme, Wim. 1998. *Medical assistance to self-settled refugees: Lessons from Guinea, 1990–1996*. PhD diss., Institute for Tropical Medicine, Antwerp, Belgium.

Zolberg, Aristide, Astri Suhrke, and Sergio Aguayo. 1989. *Escape from violence: Conflict and the refugee crisis in the developing world*. Oxford: Oxford University Press.

6

The Role of NGOs in the Democratization Process in Postwar Sierra Leone

Fredline A. O. M'Cormack-Hale

Introduction

In January 2002, Sierra Leoneans celebrated the end of eleven years of civil conflict. However, with peace came the beginning of the momentous task of rebuilding a state that was once classified amongst the world's failed states (Reno 1997). The incumbent government inherited a state whose weakness stemmed from long before the war. Former President Siaka Stevens plundered the country for years, milking state institutions to support an extensive patron-client network. Prior to 1991, Sierra Leone was ravaged by wide-scale corruption and inefficiency, with weak institutions, crippling debts, and poor economic infrastructure. The war compounded these problems. By 2002, it had claimed the lives of an estimated fifty thousand people, displaced hundreds of thousands more, and wrought massive infrastructural, as well as emotional damage.

Among the several attempts to bring the war to an end and restore peace between the various warring parties, the Lomé Peace Accord, signed on July 7, 1999, was particularly comprehensive. Included in its emphases were a focus on good governance and measures to ensure improved democracy

I am grateful to the United States Institute for Peace for funding part of this research through the Jennings Randolph Peace Scholarship Dissertation Fellowship. Portions of this chapter appear in my dissertation, "Whose Democracy? NGOs and the Democracy Project in Postconflict Sierra Leone."

in Sierra Leone, reflective of broader international trends. For countries emerging from war, the adoption of democracy is the solution widely promoted by the international community as the antidote to further conflict, ensuring long-term peace and security (Kumar 1997; Posner 2003; Smillie and Minear 2004; de Zeeuw and Kumar 2006). During the latter years of the war, and to a growing extent, in the postwar era, Sierra Leone has been the recipient of a wide variety of international interventions aimed at rebuilding the state, strengthening institutions, and (re)constructing democracy. International actors are at the forefront of rehabilitation, contributing to and, in some instances, driving the postwar reconstruction agenda, with nongovernmental organizations (NGOs) playing an integral role. While the term NGO encompasses a wide variety of meanings, the term, as applied here, refers to officially established organizations with professional and salaried staffs. It encompasses international, national, or regional organizations with external funding from mostly international sources. As such, NGOs are distinct from local and grassroots organizations.

The purpose of this chapter is to explore the impact NGOs have on democratization ten years after the Lomé accord. The central questions guiding this examination are (1) do people active in NGO programs (past or present) hold attitudes and beliefs supportive of democracy more often than those who do not participate, and (2) do they participate more in politics than those who are not involved in NGOs? To answer these questions, 416 people were sampled from seven communities in Koinadugu and Kailahun districts between July and August of 2006. Levels of political participation of individuals with varied levels of exposure to NGO activities were compared to see what impact, if any, such exposure had on political beliefs and behavior. The results are reviewed and discussed for their implications for theory and policy regarding the role of NGOs in postwar endeavors more broadly, and democratization in Sierra Leone in particular.

Building Democracy in Postconflict States

A widely accepted premise driving reconstruction initiatives in many postconflict states is that democracy is integral for the institutionalization of sustained peace (Yannis 2002; Fanthorpe 2006). To this end, countries transitioning from war are subject to a wide number of interventions aimed at (re)building democratic institutions and strengthening the state. However, this is not enough; in addition to better-functioning institutions that govern rule of law, elections, and party systems, there is a resurgence in the importance of culture—democratic institutions must be matched by a democratic culture for consolidation to take place (Diamond 1997; Linz and Stepan 1997; Diamond 1999; Pridham 2000). Consequently, many international interventions now focus on building civil society, and on teaching this society about what it means to be democratic citizens, as scholars now believe attitudes and behaviors supportive of democracy are just as important as democratic institutions and rules for democratic consolidation (Diamond 1994). Civil society, generally conceived as the "space in a society between individuals and families, on one hand, and the state or government on the other" (Carothers 1999: 209), is perceived as the arena through which such attitudes and behaviors can be cultivated. It is ostensibly the locus of change wherein citizens become politically active and informed citizenry, able to articulate their interests' vis-à-vis an adversarial state.

Given the rise in importance of the civil society concept, democracy and development assistance geared toward building civil society have mushroomed (Hearn 2000; Ottaway and Carothers 2000; Knack 2004) as both are theorized to contribute to strengthening democracy, albeit in different ways. For many donors, the ideal trajectory is the implementation of relief and rehabilitation efforts in the immediate aftermath of war, followed by economic development with political and social interventions (de Zeeuw and Kumar 2006).

It is in this latter capacity that NGOs have grown in importance, receiving recognition in recent years for their role not only in bringing about development, but also in civil society building (Hyden 1997). NGOs are perceived as working at the grassroots levels, where they are more in tune with local contexts and subsequently more effective than state organizations (Fowler 1988). NGOs with development agendas, as well as those with a more explicit focus on democratization, are both credited with the ability to build democracy in postwar states, although the mechanisms are different. One hypothesis is that by encouraging individuals to organize in community development groups, NGOs can foster civic norms; another assumes that by building or assisting civil society, NGOs contribute to democratization (Mercer 2002). In the first case, such civic engagement can give rise to norms that range from democratic values such as tolerance and trust to attitudes and beliefs supportive of democracy. In the second case, NGOs are engaged in various types of activities aimed at improving citizen's knowledge and awareness about political processes, including civic education. In so doing, NGOs can contribute to the development of a civil society that is politically informed and engaged, as knowledgeable citizens are able to articulate citizen demands and hold their government accountable.

In practice, however, the record on the impact of NGOs on democratization is mixed. Current research on the linkages between NGOs, development, and democratization has yielded contradictory results (Macdonald 1995; Tvedt 1998; Smillie 2001; Mercer 2002; Badescu, Sum, and Uslaner 2004; Knack 2004). For example, recent research from post-Communist Europe suggests that civil society assistance might be a new imperialism (Fagan 2006) contributing to the development of externally driven groups with no grassroots support (Hemment 2004). This is also echoed by Hearn and Robinson (2000), who, in their comparative work of civil society assistance in three African countries, found that while such assistance can indeed strengthen the legitimacy of democratic political institutions, funding restrictions to specific organizations often staffed by Western-educated elites constrained political participation to an elect few. Badescu, Sum, and Uslaner (2004) also note the predominance of elites: in their research in Romania and Moldova, they found that contrary to the social capital literature, civic participation, while leading to higher levels of civic engagement, trust, and tolerance on the part of elites that run organizations, did not have the same effect on the mass public. On the other hand, in Southeast Asia, it would appear that international efforts to strengthen NGOs and civil society have led to more concrete impacts on democratic developments (Quigley 2000).

Largely missing from these evaluations, however, is an examination of the influence these interventions have on micro-level political behavior, a subject of importance given renewed focus on the masses in the literature on democratic consolidation (Diamond 1999). Less is known of the effect democracy assistance has on the demand side of politics at the level of the individual, that is, of what influence it plays in shaping citizen engagement with the state, political participation, and attitudes and beliefs toward democracy. This brief overview has sought to make clear that while there is a solid body of theory dealing with democratization under stable political conditions, so far we lack a comprehensive theory of the impact of NGOs in civil-society-building and democracy strengthening in postwar states. Given this, more critical studies tracing the linkages between local-level participation in development projects and micro-level participation in the political system is needed to better understand if, and how, such linkages take place (Macdonald 1995). Moreover, although democracy assistance makes sense in countries that are politically stable, the utility of such support in countries where civil conflict or war has occurred, and where the state has shown signs of failure to cope with such strife, is less clear.

International Assistance in Postwar Sierra Leone: The Context

Sierra Leone is particularly appropriate for examining the extent to which NGOs contribute to democracy strengthening in postwar contexts. As a state once designated as failed, Sierra Leone is the recipient of substantial amounts of international assistance, targeted both at development as well as democracy strengthening. Aid comes from a variety of sources, including bilateral and multilateral donors, various United Nations (UN) agencies, and NGOs. In 2006, aid assistance to Sierra Leone totaled $396.2 million, up from $286 million in 2005 (DACO 2006), with 26 percent of this assistance channeled through NGOs. NGO activity has risen steadily, growing from thirty in 1996 (Zack-Williams 1999) to over three hundred national and international NGOs[1] registered with the Ministry of Development and Economic Planning (MODEP) in 2005.

Organizations active during and immediately after the war focused mostly on emergency relief and aid, providing shelter to refugees and internally displaced persons (IDPs), food and material supply provision in camps, as well as resettlement and reintegration as areas became safe for return (Turay 2001). Short-term relief provision was soon replaced in 2003 by programs stressing long-term strategies; these have a development-oriented approach, advocating strengthening local capacities with a view toward long-term rehabilitation, with emphases in economic development, infrastructure, governance, and security (Government of Sierra Leone 2006). Democracy-building initiatives, such as institution strengthening, decentralization, civil society, and social-capital building, have more recently accompanied these programs (Smillie 2001; Government of Sierra Leone 2007), and a significant amount of aid is allocated to this sector. In 2006, $98.26 million was allocated to good governance, peace, and security, narrowly behind the amount given to human development, which, at $99.87 million, was the highest-funded category (Government of Sierra Leone 2007, 30–33).

Sierra Leone, then, provides an excellent case study in which to examine the relationship between NGO assistance and democratization. Since this country has only recently emerged from a decade of conflict, numerous international interventions have included both democratization and development components.

Operationalizing Democracy Strengthening

The central questions explored in this chapter are whether citizens engaged in projects run by NGOs (be they development or democracy oriented) are more likely to be supportive of democracy, be involved in groups and organizations (civil society), and participate more in the political arena than citizens with no NGO exposure. These questions are examined using the general term democracy strengthening (the dependent variable) to encompass attitudes and beliefs about democracy as well as political participation.

At the level of the first core-conceptual attribute—attitudes, beliefs, and awareness—two dimensions based on elements of Almond and Verba's (1963) conceptualization of political culture are used. They define political culture as "a people's predominant beliefs, attitudes, values, ideals, sentiments, and evaluations about the political system of their country and the role of the self in that system" (cited in Diamond 1999, 163). Although there is some disagreement,[2] the attitudes (first dimension) that the general public holds about democracy can be influential in determining the likelihood that democracy will persist in that country (Almond and Verba 1963; Inglehart 1990).

Also of importance is the level of citizen political awareness. This second dimension is important because for citizens to participate, they also need to be informed (Almond and Verba 1963; Bratton, Mattes, and Gyimah-Boadi 2005). For example, in their conceptualization of a "participant political culture," Almond and Verba (1963) include political interest, information, and knowledge. In the same vein, Bratton, Mattes and Gyimah-Boadi (2005, 40) find that "the quality of citizenship improves as [citizens] learn to identify their leaders, understand how the political system works, and become exposed to contemporary policy debates."

To capture "attitudes toward the political system," the following indicators are used: preference for democracy (at the abstract level) and evaluation and satisfaction with democracy (application in a specific context).[3] For the second dimension, "political awareness," the indicators used to measure awareness are knowledge of leaders and of two political concepts: democracy and decentralization.

The second core-conceptual attribute of interest is behavior in the political arena ("political behavior"). Two central dimensions are identified: "political engagement" and "civic engagement." As regime legitimacy is affected by citizen experience with democracy (Diamond 1999), citizens should value participation as a norm, as well as actively participate in politics (Inkeles 1969). Liberal conceptions of democracy hold participation as central in the democratic process, as it is the primary mechanism through which citizens can express information about their preferences, interests, and needs, as well as influence the activities of government and government response (Verba, Schlozman, and Brady 1995). Consequently, the extent to which individuals participate in the political process can signal their belief in the political system as well as form the arena in which they learn to become more democratic. In existing research, participation is often measured by looking at the following central indicators: citizen participation (measured by voter turnout), opposition participation, and former leader participation (see, for example, Lindberg 2006). However, given that the emphasis in this study is on mass participation in politics, only citizen participation is relevant. Also, as citizens can express their voice in ways other than voting, the following indicators of participation under "political engagement" (the first dimension) are incorporated: attendance at political or development meetings, contact with political leaders, and voting. Attendance at political or development meetings is measured by presence or absence at three different types of meetings open to community residents. Contact with political leaders is measured by the extent in which citizens have contacted formal and traditional leaders both in and outside of the community. Finally, voting behavior at national and local level elections is measured by looking at voter turnout records over a designated period.

The second dimension examined is civic engagement, here operationalized as membership in civic organizations and participation in collaborative community-driven development (CDD) schemes. The numbers of associations to which individuals belong is taken as a measure of civil-society activism. Empirically, the measurement of civil society covers any and all organizations in which people organize themselves for a variety of activities, including cooperative development, mutual support, and financial assistance, as well as secret-society activities.

Hypothetical Assumptions

Beliefs and behavior are modified by people's concrete experiences with the regimes in place. If these assumptions—that individual beliefs and political participation are a function of the learning that comes from exposure to NGO activity or from civil society development—are correct, the following propositions should hold true. First, at the level of attitudes and beliefs, individuals with some involvement in NGO activities will be more politically informed and more knowledgeable about political leaders and opportunities for political participation. Second, while respondents active in NGOs might be more likely to espouse abstract support for democracy, their support for democracy, in practice, will hinge on their experiences with democracy and its constituent institutions. Those who have benefited from increased political participation will be more likely to support it than those with a negative experience. The latter will be more likely to turn to alternative means, such as informal institutions, to address their problems. Third, at the level of political participation, respondents that have been exposed to NGO projects will belong to more groups and associations than other respondents. Fourth, empirically speaking, we should see greater numbers of such citizens actively participating in the political arena, attending meetings and contacting political leaders.

Methodology

A quasi-experimental approach was employed to answer the question of whether attitudes, beliefs, and political participation are affected by external interventions. Levels of political participation and attitudes and beliefs of individuals exposed to NGOs were compared to individuals unfamiliar with NGOs. Simple t-tests were conducted to ascertain whether the means of the two groups were statistically different.

Research took place in seven communities in two districts in the eastern and northern regions of Sierra Leone. Random surveys, semi-structured interviews, and focus groups were conducted with villagers above eighteen years of age at the rural community level, as well as semi-structured interviews held with heads of international- and community-based NGOs. The questionnaire included quantitative and qualitative components, with close-ended as well as open-ended questions allowing respondents to give details of their attitudes and beliefs, as well as reasons for participation. Also, the recording of other information, including socioeconomic variables and political history, allowed for more contextualization of research findings, as well as the use of constants to better establish causality.

Research Site Selection

Districts were selected using a most-different systems design (MDSD). The MDSD approach (Przeworski and Teune 1982) entailed the comparison of regions with dissimilar histories in order to conduct systematic comparisons and to control for confounding variables. The two districts, Kailahun and Koinadugu, were both affected by the war, but with different levels of severity. Kailahun was a chief rebel base during the war, and given its proximity to the diamond industry, it experienced destruction rates of up to 80 percent, as rebels burned down dwellings to discourage people from returning and to ensure their control of diamond fields. As one of the areas most affected by the war, Kailahun received intense NGO attention, primarily in the form of community-driven development (CDD) activities, including reconstruction and rehabilitation initiatives. Specifically, projects in the selected regions have had health, agriculture, economic, and educational components, and cover a variety of activities. More recently, Kailahun has been the site of activities aimed at building democracy, and thus is a good location to test the activities of NGOs concerned with providing material as well as intangible benefits.

On the other hand, Koinadugu had about 44 percent structural damage at war's end, given the remoteness of the region and difficulty of accessibility. As a result of this, as well as lower levels of destruction, Koinadugu also did not greatly benefit from postwar relief efforts. However, such marginalization originates from before the war. The largest district in Sierra Leone, Koinadugu is also among the least developed, with an extremely poor road system. Consequently, it is on the outskirts of most development interventions by the state as well as by international actors. Cultural attitudes are also among the most conservative here; Koinadugu until recently was the only district without any female political representation, whereas Kailahun had the most representation (Irin 2009). The two districts also vary in terms of predominant ethnic groups. According to the most recent census conducted in 2004, over 80 percent of residents in Kailahun are Mende, whereas Koinadugu is more ethnically mixed, with Yalunka, Fullah, and Limba residents, among others.[4]

Discussion of Findings

To get a sense of the data before turning to general distributions of the dependent variable, the overall distribution of socioeconomic variables is covered first.

Frequency Distribution of Demographic Variables

The key demographic indicators collected for this research were gender, ethnicity, religion, age, education, and occupation. There were a total of 218 males and 198 females interviewed in the survey. Mendes formed the largest bulk of respondents (53.9 percent), followed by Yalunka (36.7 percent), Fullah (5.8 percent), and others (3.5 percent). The bulk of respondents were Muslim (89.7 percent), compared to respondents that identified as Christian (10.2 percent). A total of 73.6 respondents had no formal education, 11.8 percent had received some level of Junior Secondary School (JSS) training, and 3.4 percent had attended Senior Secondary School (SSS). Some 2.4 percent said they had received some type of vocational training. The most frequently reported occupation was farming (82.4 percent), followed by students and traders (at 4.2 percent each). Business (2.2 percent) and carpentry (1.5 percent) were also represented.

The largest category of respondents was found amongst those aged 35 to 39 (12.7 percent), followed by 40 to 44 (11.7 percent). Two age groups, 25 to 29 and 45 to 49 had an equal number of respondents (11.4 percent).

Impact of NGO Participation on Democracy Strengthening: An Overview of the Distribution of the Dependent Variable

This section examines the impact that participation in NGOs has on the various components of the democracy-strengthening variable at the level of attitudes, beliefs, and behaviors. The central hypothesis of this study is that exposure to NGO projects results in strengthened democracy, measured at the level of attitudes, beliefs, and behaviors of individuals. In this section, the impact of NGO participation on these two components of democracy strengthening is explored to examine whether this is indeed the case.

Attitudes and Beliefs: The Political System

The majority of respondents held largely favorable perceptions of democracy in principle (94.9 percent indicated they preferred democracy to any other political system), with smaller percentages expressing favorable opinions of democracy in practice (42.6 percent believed Sierra Leone was a full democracy, and 56.7 percent expressed some level of positive evaluation of democracy). However, to what extent does participation or lack of participation in NGO activities influence preference for democracy, evaluation of democracy, and satisfaction with democracy?

Using a t-test to measure whether differences exist in the means of NGO participants and non-NGO participants, there were indeed significant differences in the means within some categories. On the question of how much of a democracy Sierra Leone is, respondents that had not participated in NGO projects[5] were more likely to indicate a preference for democracy than participants active in NGO projects.[6] Additionally, the group that participated in NGO projects[7] was less likely to be satisfied with democracy than their peers.[8]

Overall, however, only a minority of respondents (across both categories) said a nondemocratic government was preferable in certain situations (3.6 percent) or felt that "to people like me it doesn't matter what form of government we have" (2.0 percent). This allows us to infer that a majority of Sierra Leoneans do indeed support democracy, similar to Bratton, Mattes, and Gyimah-Boadi's (2005) findings that democracy enjoys popular support especially in countries recently undergoing multiparty elections. Thus it would appear that regardless of participation in NGOs, citizens in Sierra Leone, like many other citizens across Africa, hold the principle of democracy dear.

Endorsement of democracy in practice is less enthusiastic. There is a clear demarcation here between respondents that have been exposed to NGOs and those that have not participated in NGO programs or projects. Respondents in the former category are less likely to express satisfaction with the way in which democracy operates in Sierra Leone than those in the latter category, a difference that was statistically significant using Fisher's exact test.[9] A total of 74 percent of respondents that had not participated in NGO projects expressed satisfaction with democracy, compared to 61.4 percent of respondents with NGO exposure. Similarly, using chi-square tests to uncover association (note, these tests do not assume causality), the percentage of respondents that believed Sierra Leone was a full democracy differed depending on NGO participation,[10] with respondents exposed to NGOs less likely to believe this to be the case (34 percent compared to 52 percent).

Attitudes and Beliefs: Political Awareness

This section considers the impact of NGO participation on political awareness (operationalized specifically as knowledge of leaders and of the political concepts democracy and decentralization).

Knowledge of Leaders

Respondents were asked whether they knew the names of their paramount chief, ward councilors, members of parliament, vice president, and president. Indigenous leaders were included since traditional political institutions are also a central aspect of politics in African countries, and such leaders are often an integral part of any political system (Bratton, Mattes, and Gyimah-Boadi 2005). Findings indicate that knowledge of indigenous leaders (paramount chief and section chiefs) is high across both sets of respondents. This parallels the findings of Bratton, Mattes and Gyimah-Boadi (2005), who note that Africans are more likely to contact traditional leaders for community problems than elected representatives. It also reinforces the idea that knowledge of leaders is an important precursor to contact, implying that people are more likely to contact people with whom they are familiar. These findings also echo Verba, Schlozman, and Brady (1995), who find, in their study of U.S. politics, that personal acquaintance with public officials increases the likelihood that citizens contact these officials, and that the relative accessibility of local officials increases the likelihood that they are known by respondents.

Knowledge of elected political leaders in formal institutions was much lower. Knowledge about councilors was low overall, and NGO participation made little or no difference. NGO participation also did not make a significant difference in knowledge of ward councilors. On the other hand, NGO participation made an impact on knowledge of elected leaders at the national level, specifically the vice president (VP), member of parliament (MP), and president. Respondents with NGO exposure were more likely to name these politicians correctly. Of respondents not active in any NGO projects, 29.7 percent could correctly name the VP compared to 75.6 percent of respondents exposed to NGOs. A similar trend was observed for the office of the president. Although more people overall were able to correctly give the president's name, for respondents that had not participated in NGO projects, 57.3 percent were able to correctly name the president as compared to 96.7 percent of respondents exposed to NGO projects.

Knowledge of Political Concepts

Respondents with exposure to NGOs were more likely to have heard of the word "democracy," and be able to attribute a meaning to the term (80.1 percent of respondents active with NGOs knew the term, compared to 53.3 percent of respondents with no NGO exposure).[11] The same was true of the concept of "decentralization": 32.5 percent of respondents with exposure to NGOs had heard of the term, compared to 10.7 percent of respondents in the former category.[12]

Political Behavior: Political Engagement

Political (development) meetings are a primary mechanism through which individuals can impact development and change in their communities as well as hold officials accountable.

Attendance at Political Meetings

While political meetings provide a good opportunity to be active in the community, the study revealed that overall knowledge of ward committee meetings and district council meetings was low and knowledge of, and attendance at, these meetings was not significantly affected by NGO exposure.

On the other hand, at the community level, attendance at village development committee (VDC) meetings, while originally relatively high, increases even more depending on exposure to NGO projects. A total of

39.4 percent of respondents with no exposure to NGOs said they attended VDC meetings. This increases to 52.1 percent for respondents who have had some contact with NGOs. This suggests that while NGOs might have some impact on people's willingness to be active in development programs in their communities, respondents still prefer that local problems and issues are solved at the local level through informal rather than formal channels, like the ward and local councils established by the state.

Contact with Political Leaders
Study findings indicate that respondents were twice as likely to contact indigenous leaders and local community groups than formal ones. This feature is consistent among respondents with NGO exposure as well as those who have not participated in any NGO projects. Although respondents in the former category reported contacting chiefs, mammy queens, and local community groups more than those in the latter category, the differences were not significant. These findings are again consistent with those of Bratton, Mattes, and Gyimah-Boadi (2005), who find that Afrobarometer[13] respondents across all surveyed countries are more likely to contact traditional political leaders rather than formal elected ones to address problems in their communities. In this study, NGO participation did not significantly influence contact of formal political leaders, whether it was members of parliament, district councilors, or ward committee members.

Voting
Participation or nonparticipation in NGO activities had very little impact on whether people voted in the presidential and parliamentary elections as well as in local council elections. In the 2002 presidential and parliamentary elections, over 70 percent of respondents in both categories said they voted. Turnout for the local council elections in 2004 was lower in both categories, averaging about 50 percent, but there was no significant difference across these categories.

Political Behavior: Civic Engagement

Participation in voluntary associations and community-driven development activities can ostensibly serve as a training ground for citizens to inculcate civic norms, and to hone skills necessary to engage in the political world. To what extent are citizens exposed to NGOs more likely to participate in voluntary associations, and to participate in activities aimed at developing their communities?

Membership in Civic Organizations
Respondents with NGO experience were more likely to belong to more groups than those not exposed to these organizations. Only 10 percent of respondents with some NGO contact did not belong to any group at all, compared to 38.6 percent of respondents with no NGO contact.[14] Additionally, respondents in the former category were more likely to belong to more groups than those without NGO exposure.

Participation in Community-driven Development
Respondents with NGO exposure were significantly more likely to participate in CDD activities in their communities than those without NGO exposure, with 85 percent of those in the former category participating compared to 69.4 percent of respondents without NGO exposure.[15]

Conclusion: Toward an Understanding of NGO Impact on Democracy Strengthening

The results of the analyses seem to indicate that participation in NGO projects affects attitudes, beliefs, and political behavior to some degree: participants exposed to NGOs report higher levels of political and civic engagement. They are in greater contact with political leaders, attend more political and development meetings, belong to more community associations, and participate in greater numbers in community-driven development activities in their communities.

In terms of attitudes or beliefs about democracy, however, the results are more mixed. These respondents are less likely to evaluate democracy positively, and are less satisfied with democracy than their counterparts who have no NGO experience. Nevertheless, they have greater knowledge of leaders, as well as political concepts, all of which are potentially influential in making informed evaluations about the way in which democracy works and in holding government accountable. Respondents exposed to NGOs were significantly more likely to know the name of the president and vice president, as well as the chief, but this significance disappears when considering other leaders such as the councilor and members of parliament.

Such a variety of responses are in line with the learning approach advocated here. It would appear that through the activities of NGOs, respondents are able to gain greater knowledge about the political system and also engage more with politicians. However, given that such exchanges do not necessarily bear fruit in the sense of greater responsiveness from central government and increased development at the community level, some respondents become frustrated and work more with local organizations and local leaders to get things done. In addition, this frustration leads to overall negative perceptions of democracy within the specific context of Sierra Leone. Participants active in NGOs are less likely to evaluate democracy as practiced in Sierra Leone favorably. In addition, they are less satisfied with democracy than those not exposed to NGOs.

This combination of results suggests that there is no clear answer concerning the impact of NGOs on democracy strengthening. However, some preliminary comments can be made, especially when these results are interpreted within the context of open-ended responses in the questionnaire and focus group discussions (FGDs). For instance, the increased numbers of respondents active in NGOs that are more likely to express dissatisfaction with democracy in practice becomes less surprising. Similar sentiments were expressed in a number of FGDs also. In these discussions, respondents exposed to NGOs were also more likely to have engaged in political activities, attended political meetings, and contacted political leaders. These same respondents expressed dissatisfaction with the outcome of these endeavors. As one respondent put it, "We know what to do. We know to contact our ward committees and local councils if we want development, but we have done all of these things, and nothing has happened."[16] These respondents also indicated that, through NGOs, they had learned more about the process of decentralization. As a result, they were familiar with the official mechanisms through which development was to take place in the community. However, while aware of these processes, their general perception is that these formal avenues are largely ineffective. Furthermore, when asked about reasons for voting, many cited the limitations of the local councilors and frustration with the slow pace of development in their communities. Respondents perceived councilors as far removed from their communities and uninterested in bringing about greater community development.

In view of this, respondents were more likely to turn to local influential elites for development, and to organize themselves in groups to implement development projects in their communities. Thus, participation in civic associations and community-driven development tends to be high.

While NGOs are contributing to the formation of groups through which citizens can organize in CDD and civic associations, as well as teaching citizens about their civic duties, some caution is in order. The experiment of democracy, and the makings of civic citizens, must face the reality of a nascent state, emerged, yes, from the crisis of state failure, but nevertheless still struggling to find a way to become relevant to citizens socially, economically, and politically. First, by undertaking many of the social welfare and economic development programs of the state, NGOs further contribute to the undermining of state-society relations. Respondents were more likely to seek support from an NGO, rather than the state, for a development project for their community.

Additionally, by encouraging citizens to participate and to be more active in the political realm, these organizations are contributing to possible insecurities. The state is unable to accommodate the many demands that newly empowered citizens make, possibly increasing citizen frustration as they follow the appropriate mechanisms without seeing any benefits. This could further alienate citizens from the state. During a particularly heated exchange in an FGD with youth in Kailahun, they expressed dissatisfaction with the return to "old ways" following the war. They felt that traditional leaders unfairly exacted fines and appropriated their labor without adequate compensation. Some youth openly talked about how the war at least brought some measure of equality and addressed their concerns as youth in a farming community with little prospects of earning much revenue. In a community where at least half of the youth were former ex-combatants reintegrated into their home communities following the war, such sentiments could coalesce into a return to conflict.

The policies of decentralization are a further concern. Most of the emphasis has been on introducing what, to many people, are new forms of governance and ignoring the traditional systems of leadership currently in place. This has a number of serious ramifications. First, inequities within the former system that privileged the older elite was one of the contributing factors to the war (Richards 1998). Few attempts have been made to reform this system; instead, resources are being used to create, almost from scratch, a new system of governance that has yet to claim the loyalties of people (Fanthorpe 2006). A further conflict exists between chiefs and the new political elite (local government officials) who now officially hold the keys for development of their communities. The modification of political behavior by external programs and projects is further complicated by the existence of informal institutions, that is, pre-existing incentive structures influencing behavioral change as well as socioeconomic conditions (Burnell 2000, 351). Despite the existence of newly-created forms of political leadership, traditional leaders are still perceived as the most appropriate forum for many people interested in bringing development to their communities.

The seeming contradictions of respondents active in NGOs seem to echo these problems. Although they have increased knowledge and are active in their communities, the failure of current interventions to build on indigenous institutions and existing avenues for development could undermine democratization efforts. Problems arise from the emphasis placed on formal institutions at the expense of considering on-the-ground realities and the importance that traditional institutions play in people's lives.

Successful democratization necessitates the melding of both the informal rules that structure people's lives, as well as the formal ones newly imposed by the state and donors. Otherwise, competing sources of governance (formal versus traditional institutions), combined with the low capacity of a state still recovering from war, could lead to empowered democrats exercising a powerless democratic voice and potentially sow seeds for a return to instability.[17]

Notes

1. The focus of this study is development assistance channeled through INGOs and NGOs, as they are a significant, although not the only, source of development and democracy assistance. The emphasis is largely on the role of INGOs. While NGOs are also active, they tend to be recipients of aid from the larger INGOs, rather than donors themselves, and often reflect the mandates and concerns of INGOs. For the purposes of simplicity, however, I simply use the term NGO to denote both INGOs and NGOs alike.

2. See, for example, Muller and Seligson (1994), who find that civic culture attitudes do not significantly impact changes in democracy.

3. For preference for democracy, respondents were asked, "Which statement do you agree with the most?" For evaluation of democracy, they were asked, "How much of a democracy is Sierra Leone?" For satisfaction with democracy, they were asked, "How satisfied are you with the way democracy works in Sierra Leone?" These questions are the same as those used in the Afrobarometer. The high rate of respondents who favoured the concept of democracy is comparable to Afrobarometer findings across other countries in Africa. In 12 countries in which the surveys have been implemented, 70 percent indicate a preference for democracy (Bratton, Mattes, and Gyimah-Boadi 2004). Sierra Leone is among other countries like Botswana, Tanzania, and Nigeria, where greater than 80 percent of the populace indicate a preference for democracy.

4. The official Web site for statistics on Sierra Leone is http://www.statistics.sl.

5. $X = 2.21, SD = .985$.

6. $X = 1.85, SD = .981, t (341) = .001$.

7. $X = 2.36, SD = 1.582$.

8. $X = 2.36, SD = 1.582, t (353) = .013$.

9. Categories were collapsed into satisfied and not satisfied with democracy, excluding those that expressed "no opinion," "do not know," and "no response."

10. $\chi^2 (3, N = 346) = 1.80, p < .000$.

11. $\chi^2 (1) = 2.880E1 \, p < .000$.

12. $\chi^2 (1) = 2.82E1 \, p < .000$.

13. The Afrobarometer is a research project measuring public opinion in over a dozen countries in Africa using survey methods. First launched in 2001, the barometer examines social, political, and economic attitudes over time in

African countries that meet the criteria of some measure of democratic and market reforms. Surveyed countries include Ghana, Nigeria, and South Africa.

14. p = .000.
15. $\chi 2(1) = 1.470E1$ p = .000.
16. FGD conducted with male youth group members in Ngeima, Kailahun, August 10, 2006.
17. Much of this chapter is drawn from my dissertation on NGOs in postwar Sierra Leone. Thus, this analysis presents a limited analysis irrespective of differentiation based on region, culture, and gender, among other variables, due to space constraints. For a fuller treatment, please refer to M'Cormack-Hale (2008).

References

Almond, Gabriel A., and Sidney Verba. 1963. *The civic culture: Political attitudes and democracy in five nations*. Princeton: Princeton University Press.

Badescu, Gabriel, Paul Sum, and Eric M. Uslaner. 2004. Civil society development and democratic values in Romania and Moldova. *East European Politics & Societies* 18 (2): 316–41.

Bratton, Michael, Robert B. Mattes, and Emmanuel Gyimah-Boadi, eds. 2005. *Public opinion, democracy, and market reform in Africa*. Cambridge: Cambridge University Press.

Burnell, Peter J. 2000. *Democracy assistance: International co-operation for democratization*. London: Frank Cass.

Carothers, Thomas. 1999. *Aiding democracy abroad: The learning curve*. Washington, DC: Carnegie Endowment for International Peace.

Diamond, Larry. 1994. Rethinking civil society: Toward democratic consolidation. *Journal of Democracy* 5 (3): 4–18.

———. ed. 1997. *Consolidating the third wave democracies: Themes and perspectives*. Baltimore: Johns Hopkins University Press.

———. 1999. *Developing democracy: Toward consolidation*. Baltimore: Johns Hopkins University Press.

Fagan, Adam. 2006. Transnational aid for civil society development in post-socialist Europe: Democratic consolidation or a new imperialism? *Journal of Communist Studies and Transition Politics* 22 (1): 115–34.

Fanthorpe, Richard. 2006. On the limits of liberal peace: Chiefs and democratic decentralization in postwar Sierra Leone. *African Affairs* 105 (418): 27–49.

Fowler, A. 1988. Nongovernmental organizations in Africa: Achieving comparative advantage in relief and micro-development. Discussion paper 249, Institute of Development Studies, Brighton.

Government of Sierra Leone. 2006. Development assistance to Sierra Leone 2004–2005. Development Assistance Cooperation Office (DACO). http://www.daco-sl.org/reports/Dev_ass_rep04-05.pdf.

Government of Sierra Leone. 2007. Development Assistance to Sierra Leone 2006. Development Assistance Cooperation Office (DACO). http://www.daco-sl.org/reports/Dev_ass_rep06.pdf.

Hearn, Julie. 2000. Aiding democracy? Donors and civil society in South Africa. *Third World Quarterly* 21 (5): 815–30.

Hearn, Julie, and Mark Robinson. 2000. Civil society and democracy assistance in Africa. In *Democracy assistance: International co-operation for democratization*, ed. P. J. Burnell, 241–62. London: Frank Cass.

Hemment, J. 2004. The riddle of the third sector: Civil society, international aid, and NGOs in Russia. *Anthropological Quarterly* 77 (2): 215–41.

Hyden, Goran. 1997. Civil society, social capital, and development: Dissection of a complex discourse. *Studies in Comparative International Development* 32 (1): 3–30.

Irin Humanitartian News and Analysis. 2009. Sierra Leone: Women access power, vote by vote. http://www.irinnews.org/Report.aspx?ReportId=83393.

Inglehart, Ronald. 1990. *Culture shift in advanced industrial society*. Princeton: Princeton University Press.

Inkeles, A. 1969. Participant citizenship in six developing countries. *American Political Science Review* 63 (4): 1120–41.

Knack, Stephen. 2004. Does foreign aid promote democracy? *International Studies Quarterly* 48 (1): 251–66.

Kumar, Krishna. 1997. *Rebuilding societies after civil war: Critical roles for international assistance*. Boulder, CO: Lynne Rienner.

Lindberg, Staffan I. 2006. The surprising significance of African elections. *Journal of Democracy* 17 (1): 140–51.

Linz, Juan J., and Alfred C. Stepan. 1997. Toward consolidated democracies. In *Consolidating the third wave democracies: Themes and perspectives*, ed. L. J. Diamond, 14–33. Baltimore: Johns Hopkins University Press.

Macdonald, L. 1995. NGOs and the problematic discourse of participation: Cases from Costa Rica. In *Debating development discourse: Institutional and popular perspectives*, ed. D. B. Moore and G. J. Schmitz, 201–29. New York: St. Martin's.

M'Cormack-Hale, Fredline A. O. 2008. Whose democracy? NGOs and the democracy project in postconflict Sierra Leone. PhD diss., University of Florida.

Mercer, Claire. 2002. NGOs, civil society and democratization: A critical review of the literature. *Progress in Development Studies* 2 (1): 5–22.

Muller, Edward N., and Mitchell A. Seligson. 1994. Civic culture and democracy: The question of causal relationships. *American Political Science Review* 88 (3): 635–52.

Ottaway, Marina, and Thomas Carothers. 2000. *Funding virtue: Civil society aid and democracy promotion*. Washington, DC: Carnegie Endowment for International Peace.

Posner, Daniel N. 2003. Civil society and the reconstruction of failed states. In *When states fail: Causes and consequences*, ed. R. I. Rotberg, 237–55. Princeton: Princeton University Press.

Pridham, Geoffrey. 2000. *The dynamics of democratization: A comparative approach.* London: Continuum.

Przeworski, Adam, and Henry Teune. 1982. *The logic of comparative social inquiry.* Malabar, FL: R. E. Krieger.

Quigley, Kevin F. F. 2000. Democracy assistance in south-east Asia: Long history/unfinished business. In *Democracy assistance: International co-operation for democratization*, ed. P. J. Burnell, 263–87. London: Frank Cass.

Reno, William. 1997. *Humanitarian emergencies and warlord economies in Liberia and Sierra Leone.* Helsinki, Finland: UNU World Institute for Development Economics Research (UNU/WIDER).

Richards, Paul. 1998. *Fighting for the rain forest: War, youth & resources in Sierra Leone.* Portsmouth, NH: Heinemann.

Smillie, Ian, ed. 2001. *Patronage or partnership: Local capacity building in humanitarian crises.* Bloomfield, CT: Kumarian Press.

Smillie, Ian, and Larry Minear. 2004. *The charity of nations: Humanitarian action in a calculating world.* Bloomfield, CT: Kumarian Press.

Turay, T. M. 2001. Sierra Leone: Peace building in purgatory. In *Patronage or partnership: Local capacity building in humanitarian crises*, ed. Ian Smillie, 157–74. Bloomfield, CT: Kumarian Press.

Tvedt, Terje. 1998. *Angels of mercy or development diplomats? NGOs and foreign aid.* Trenton: Africa World Press.

Verba, Sidney, Kay Lehman Schlozman, and Henry E. Brady. 1995. *Voice and equality: Civic voluntarism in American politics.* Cambridge, MA: Harvard University Press.

Yannis, Alexandros. 2002. State collapse and its implications for peace-building and reconstruction. *Development & Change* 33 (5): 817–35.

Zack-Williams, Alfred B. 1999. Sierra Leone: The political economy of civil war, 1991–98. *Third World Quarterly* 20 (1): 143–62.

Zeeuw, Jeroen de, and Krishna Kumar, eds. 2006. *Promoting democracy in postconflict societies.* Boulder, CO: Lynne Rienner.

7

Sierra Leone's Development Challenges

Victor A. B. Davies

Introduction

This chapter focuses on the economic aspects of Sierra Leone's development challenges in the post-Lomé and postwar era. Sierra Leone's overarching development challenge over the years has been to manage a rich natural resource base to raise the quality of life for its overwhelmingly poor population. The civil war has reinforced this challenge and added the imperative of peacebuilding. Raising living standards and consolidating the peace would require pro-poor economic growth with employment creation, making economic policy central to the challenge. Pro-poor growth would generate the resources required to raise living standards. Employment creation for the country's predominantly youthful population is an urgent priority in order to consolidate the peace by absorbing abundant unemployed labor, including former combatants. Virtually all explanations of the conflict point to youth alienation and marginalization as a major culprit (Abdallah 1997; Richards 2005; and Peters 2006). Employment creation would help address youth alienation.

Sierra Leone is endowed with potentially favorable conditions for pro-poor economic growth with employment creation. It has minerals—diamonds, rutile, bauxite, and gold; agricultural and marine resources; and considerable tourism potential. It is a coastal country, implying potentially low transport costs to overseas markets. Ironically, however, Sierra Leone has been one of the poorest countries on the globe, ranking in the bottom five of the United Nations Development Program (UNDP) Human Development Index (2007) over the years. Over 70 percent of the population lives below the poverty line of US $1 a day. The war has worsened matters.

This chapter focuses on the following key economic aspects of Sierra Leone's development challenge: economic management, public sector reform, natural resource management, private sector development, rural development, and the need for economic transformation.

Macroeconomic Management

Sound macroeconomic management—management of the economy as a whole—promotes economic development. Macroeconomic mismanagement was a key feature of the patrimonial system of governance blamed for the war (Reno 1995; Davies 2007). Following years of economic crisis and decline, a structural adjustment program was launched in 1989. Economic reforms have been pursued ever since, even during the war. The reforms have sought to stabilize the economy—that is, reduce inflation—promote private sector-led growth, and reduce the hitherto pervasive role of government in the economy. Markets were liberalized in the early 1990s. The exchange rate was floated and interest rates were deregulated. The Poverty Reduction and Growth Facility (PRGF) with the International Monetary Fund (IMF) provides the current framework for macroeconomic reforms. In 2005, a Poverty Reduction Strategy Paper (PRSP) was launched. The PRSP is a three-year (2005–2007) plan; each year's plan is comprised of three pillars, with objectives closely tied to the Millennium Development Goals. The government is currently preparing a second PRSP. Sierra Leone reached the Highly Indebted Poor Countries (HIPC) completion point in 2006 and became eligible for substantial debt relief. The government has adopted the Medium Term Expenditure Framework (MTEF)—a three-year rolling budget.

Some progress has been realized in generating postwar growth, although it is not clear whether this is pro-war. Figure 7.1 shows a rebound of postwar per capita income after the decline of the prewar and wartime years. Sierra Leone's growth rate averaged 7.6 percent in the 2002 through 2006 period. However, per capita income remains low. It was only US$228 in 2006, compared with US$290 in the early 1980s. Moreover, a high degree of inequality underlies the low per capita income. Sierra Leone has one of the highest levels of income inequality in the world, as reflected in a Gini Index of 63 percent.

Civil war generates capital flight, which, if reversed postwar, could promote investment and growth. Thus, postconflict economic policy should seek to encourage flight capital repatriation. The macroeconomic and political environment would determine how much of the flight capital is repatriated, if any. Davies (2008) finds that low inflation

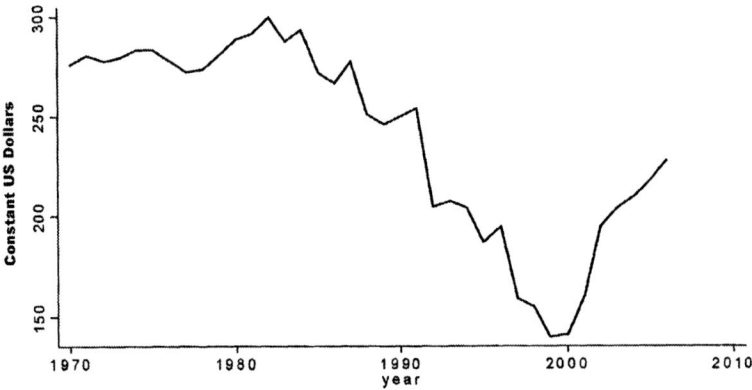

Figure 7.1   Sierra Leone's per capita income.

encourages postwar flight capital repatriation. More generally, a favorable investment climate would induce flight capital repatriation. I give more details on Sierra Leone's investment climate in the discussion on private sector development.

Civil war also induces human capital flight, producing a large diaspora by the end of the conflict. Although reliable statistics are not available, it is generally believed that the United States and United Kingdom host a large Sierra Leonean diaspora (International Crisis Group 2008). The diaspora constitutes a resource base for economic development. Notably, it could be encouraged to invest in the domestic economy and to fill gaps in human resource needs.

Low revenue mobilization, high aid dependence and a weak financial sector are key constraints to economic management in Sierra Leone. I examine these in turn.

Low-revenue Mobilization

Generating revenues to run the state is a key function of any government. Government revenue-generating capacity had virtually collapsed prior to the war in Sierra Leone. Domestic revenues plummeted from 17 percent of GDP in the 1970s to 8 percent from 1985 through 1989. The fiscal collapse was probably one of the immediate causes of state failure: it denied the state the resources to govern. Sierra Leone's challenge is to generate substantial fiscal revenues from a potentially large revenue base comprised of minerals and marine resources.

Some revenue-enhancing measures have been instituted postwar. In 2003, the two main revenue-collection institutions—the Customs and Excise Department and the Income Tax Department—were merged under the aegis of the National Revenue Authority, charged with responsibility for collecting all duties, taxes, revenues, and penalties, as prescribed by the laws of Sierra Leone. Thus, the authority has assumed all revenue collection responsibilities previously performed by a plethora of institutions. This is expected to help to reduce leakages, improve public oversight and monitoring, and reduce the transactions costs of revenue collection.

Tax revenues averaged 12.7 percent of GDP in 2002 through 2006 period, compared with 7.9 percent from 1996 through 1999 (Table 7.1). However, tax revenues have been declining from a peak of 15.2 percent in 2003 to 11 percent in 2006. This suggests a reversal of the early gains in raising revenue-generation capacity.

Revenue collection in Sierra Leone faces several issues. First is the smuggling of imports across the border with Guinea due to lower tariffs there. Guinea's implementation of a regional common external tariff, which Sierra Leone started to implement in 2005, might reduce the incentive for smuggling. However, the common external tariff could decrease tax revenues since it lowers the rates for trade taxes, Sierra Leone's principal source of tax revenues.

Table 7.1 Tax revenues and foreign aid

Year	Tax revenue (% Gross Domestic Product)	Foreign aid (% Gross National Income)
1992–95	10.8	28
1996–99	7.9	16
Average (2002–06)	12.7	34
2000	10.8	30
2001	13.6	44
2002	14.0	39
2003	15.2	32
2004	12.2	35
2005	11.1	29
2006	11	25

Source: Tax revenue: Ministry of Finance, Freetown. Foreign aid: World Development Indicators (September 2009).

Second, the government is undertaking fiscal decentralization as part of a wider decentralization program. Fiscal decentralization might raise the volume of fiscal revenues and the efficiency of fiscal expenditures with the direct involvement of local stakeholders. However, there is scope for corruption at the local level, far from Freetown, where attention is usually focused. Human resource constraints could also emerge.

Third, taxation tends to punish visible investment. Tax liability is often judged on the basis of physical capital in the absence of reliable accounting records, providing an incentive to underinvest in physical capital to escape taxation. This, in turn, could hurt economic growth.

Fourth, the government is replacing the sales tax with a value-added tax, claiming that the new tax would improve the cash flow of businesses and reduce multiple taxation (Government of Sierra Leone Budget Statement for 2008). However, concerns have been raised in the literature about the efficacy of a value-added tax in countries with a large informal sector like Sierra Leone.

Finally, the government intends to renegotiate tax and duty concessions as "most of these were negotiated from a position of weakness especially after the war when economic conditions were uncertain ... some of these concessions have had a distorting effect on the investment environment while others are being abused" (Government of Sierra Leone 2007, 49).

Aid Dependence

Sierra Leone has been highly aid dependent. Foreign aid financed some 50 percent of the government budget between 2001 and 2006. Furthermore, weak government institutional capacity has resulted in reliance on foreign experts for policy formulation and management. The cost of aid dependence includes considerable donor influence in economic management at the expense of national ownership. Aid flows are volatile while shortfalls and delays are common. The government sometimes responds to the shortfalls and delays by borrowing from the domestic banking system through open-market operations such as the purchase and sale of government security. However, open-market operations in these circumstances lead to high treasury bill interest rates relative to commercial bank rates. In 2004, interest rates on treasury bills exceeded commercial banks' lending rates. This creates a disincentive for commercial banks to lend to the public, which, in turn, could hurt investment and growth. Moreover, high treasury bill rates raise the cost of government borrowing. Domestic interest payments were as high as 16 percent of domestic revenues in 2007. Aid flows also come with high administrative costs for the government. The government of Sierra Leone Budget Statement for 2007 (53) declared that "budget support from our development partners have been tied to different sets of standards by the different donors, with varying timeframes. This has led not only to increasing the transaction cost for the purpose of reporting and accommodating donor missions, but has also engendered unpredictability and volatility in donor inflows, resulting in difficulties in planning and budgeting."

Weak Financial Sector

Sierra Leone's financial sector is rudimentary and fragmented, with a small formal sector and a large informal sector. The formal sector is urban based and bank dominated. As of 2009, there were about thirteen commercial banks, five community banks (formerly rural banks), a national cooperative development bank, a post office savings bank, a housing cooperation, a finance and trust corporation, a discount house, a home finance company, eight insurance companies, and forty-four foreign exchange bureaus. Informal institutions, such as traditional moneylenders and savings and rotating societies, are ubiquitous.

A narrow financial sector offers little scope to use monetary policy as a tool for economic management. Furthermore, it impedes savings mobilization and access to finance, especially for small and medium enterprises and rural operatives. Commercial bank lending goes mainly to commerce and mining. Community banks are expected to provide concessional financial services to local communities.

The Public Sector

The public sector performs a critical role in the development process. It is responsible for formulating and implementing government policy, collecting and spending government revenues, and delivering basic services like health and education. Prior to the war, Sierra Leone's public sector systematically disintegrated to the point of collapse. A wide range of institutional reforms has been pursued postwar. Some public enterprises have been privatized or liquidated. The government has launched a public financial management program to improve the policy-making, budget-preparation, and procurement processes.

We now turn to corruption and service delivery, major problems facing the public sector.

Corruption

Corruption is generally perceived as a serious problem in Sierra Leone. The country ranked 150 out of 180 on the Transparency International Corruption Perception Index (CPI) in 2007. The CPI rank is derived on the basis of a CPI score, which relates to perceptions of the degree of corruption in a country as viewed by business people and country analysts. The score ranges from zero (highly corrupt) to ten (highly clean). Transparency International interprets a score of less than three as a sign of rampant corruption. Sierra Leone's score ranged between 2.1 and 2.4 from 2003 through 2007. Evidence of corruption also comes from the Public Expenditure Tracking Survey (PETS), which tracks expenditures from government ministries in Freetown to regional and district offices. PETS surveys in 2001 revealed that resources transferred to provincial offices are negligible relative to the allocations in Freetown. A 2003 survey reported that schools received only 45 percent of disbursed government-fee subsidies, while medical officers received less than 10 percent of essential drugs sent to them.

An Anti-Corruption Commission was set up in 2000. Through January 2007, forty-two cases were investigated and referred to court, including a case against a hospital payroll officer and another against a headmaster. However, only seven convictions were secured. Only a few high-profile cases have been prosecuted (IMF 2006). The public perception is that corruption is rampant and the Anti-Corruption Commission is ineffective, eschewing high-profile cases (IMF 2007).

Service Delivery

Efficient service delivery is essential for poverty alleviation and for improving human welfare. As stated, in Sierra Leone, tracking surveys reveal that corruption is a major problem in public service delivery. The present institutional framework for service delivery accords a major role to government: it is solely responsible for policy management and financing, and is the major provider of retail services. Given weak government institutions, the present policy of combining policy management, financing, and retail service delivery appears to be inappropriate: The government is not well placed to engage in large-scale retail service delivery. Greater private participation is recommended in order to raise efficiency through competition and specialization. There is already a large degree of de facto privatization: government health units and schools are run as if they were private entities by government-paid operators who charge and retain fees and also receive (and sometimes misappropriate) government funding. This is, of course, a perverse and corrupt form of privatization. But it is the type of privatization that is more or less inevitable in situations when weak public institutions attempt to engage in large-scale retail service delivery in addition to policy management and financing. Formalizing privatization would eliminate corruption and encourage the participation of, and competition among, bona fide private suppliers.

Natural Resource Management

Managing Sierra Leone's natural resources—diamonds, rutile, bauxite, gold, and rich marine resources—lies at the heart of Sierra Leone's development challenge. Key concerns include Sierra Leone's capacity to negotiate favorable terms with exploitation and exploration companies, corruption, provision of basic information about the resources, and the ability to police the resources. Diamonds have been the most important natural resource, for good or ill. Diamonds are found in two types of deposits—alluvial and kimberlite. Through 2003, only alluvial deposits were exploited. Alluvial diamonds have played an ambiguous role in Sierra Leone's development process. In the 1960s and 1970s, they accounted for some 15 percent of GDP and 70 percent of official export earnings. However, over the years, smuggling has been widespread. Diamonds helped criminalize economic activity, especially in the 1980s in the face of widespread black markets and shortages of basic commodities induced by extensive government intervention in markets. The diamonds were smuggled abroad and the proceeds used to purchase scarce essential imports for sale in local black markets. Subsequently, diamonds helped sustain the war by providing financing for the rebellion and producing a war-prolonging congruence of interests among the protagonists (Davies 2000).

Policing alluvial diamond deposits is difficult because they are widely dispersed—over an area of eighteen thousand square kilometers in Sierra Leone—and can be mined with simple tools, facilitating illicit mining and smuggling. In the postwar period, the government participates in the global Kimberley Diamond Certification Process, which aims to prevent the trade in "conflict diamonds," and in the Extractive Industries Transparency Initiative, which seeks to improve governance in resource-rich countries through the publication of company payments and government revenues from natural resources. Official diamond exports increased from US$10 million in 2000 to about US$230 million in 2008. However, the challenge is for Sierra Leone to benefit substantially from its alluvial diamonds. Fiscal revenues, which come from license fees and a 3 percent export tax, are relatively low. Postwar, they have amounted to less than US$10 million despite the improved official exports. Taxes and other charges are low to reduce the incentive for illicit mining and smuggling, perennial problems facing the diamond industry.

Reports point to widespread poverty among laborers, suggesting that diamond mining could be immiserizing (United States Agency for International Development 2001). Many laborers see the mines as their only chance out of poverty, and they are prepared to gamble on a life-changing diamond find. Typically, they are engaged by financiers who provide mining equipment and food on credit. The laborers share any profit from their findings with their financiers, who are mostly foreigners, mainly of Lebanese origin (Moyers 2003). However, the chances of a significant diamond find are low. Thus, many laborers end up poorer than they would have been elsewhere.

The fact of low government fiscal revenues and widespread poverty among laborers suggests that the diamond resources are of limited benefit to the people of Sierra Leone. Moreover, diamonds still pose a threat to peace. Many former combatants, faced with unemployment, have returned to the diamond mines (Peters 2006). Maintaining law and order in the mines has always been challenging even in the best of times. Violent clashes have been occurring over mineral rights in the postwar period through 2008.

There is no simple solution to the problem of how to manage Sierra Leone's alluvial diamond resources to generate widespread benefit. For instance, the United States Agency for International Development (USAID) funded a cooperative credit scheme for the diamond laborers, attributing the laborers' destitution to lack of finance and diamond-valuation knowledge. However, the recovery rate has been low, less than 20 percent in 2005 (Levin and Gberie 2006).

Large-scale mining holds better prospects for fiscal revenues. However, enforcing property rights to permit large-scale mining may be difficult. Some mining plants have been invaded and occupied by disgruntled youths. Mining of kimberlite diamond deposits started in 2004. Being spatially concentrated and requiring huge capital outlays, kimberlite deposits are not susceptible to illicit mining like alluvial deposits, offering better fiscal revenues prospects.

Rutile and bauxite were the leading sources of tax revenues and official foreign exchange earnings when the war forced the closure of the mines in 1994. Mining operations resumed in 2007. Sierra Leone has considerable marine resources with a 560-kilometer-long coastline. The government of Sierra Leone's 2007 budget statement (22) cites "inadequate monitoring and policing of our offshore waters, resulting in illegal shipping and transshipment" as a major problem facing the industry. One option to consider is auctions for industrial fishing. This would not affect artisanal fishing, which does not operate in the same fishing zones.

Peace opens up the scope for commercial exploitation of previously unexploited resources, reinforcing the need to provide a suitable environment, including provision of basic information, for the exploitation of the natural resources. Also, the government may wish to invest in cadastre systems, as it has already done for alluvial diamond deposits, to reduce uncertainties. It would also be necessary to establish a tax structure, which, while leaving extraction profitable (to firms), captures a substantial share of the profits for government.

Private-sector Development

The private sector lies at the heart of economic development in Sierra Leone, given the market orientation of the economy. The private sector already dominates the economy, accounting for over 95 percent of GDP. Most sectors of the economy are entirely private, including agriculture (including fisheries), manufacturing, mining, construction, and mobile telephony. The private sector dominates other sectors like transportation and hoteling. Moreover, as argued earlier, there is a need to allow greater private participation in retail service delivery in health and education.

The constraints to private sector development in Sierra Leone are formidable. Infrastructure is poor. Electricity supply, water supply, and fixed-line telephony have been poor, even in Freetown, the national capital. Since the beginning of 2008, the new government of President Ernest Koroma has, to an extent, improved electricity supply in the capital city of Freetown. The Bumbuna hydroelectric project, completed in 2009, has a peak capacity of 50 megawatts during the rainy season, falling to as low as 18 megawatts during the dry season. The estimated current demand in Freetown, the main beneficiary, is 40 megawatts. Freetown also faces severe traffic congestion problems due to a poor road network. Furthermore, the country's only international airport is located on a peninsula away from Freetown. Traveling between Freetown and the airport, which is only a few miles away but is not connected directly by road, is often problematic. Helicopters and sea modes of transport are commonly used. Helicopter travel has been a risky proposition, while the ferry service, the main means of sea travel, is erratic. There is an urgent need to address this matter.

A weak institutional environment for business also constrains private sector development. Sierra Leone ranked 160 out of 178 countries on the World Bank "doing business index" for 2007. The index ranks economies on their ease of doing business, one being the best rank. The index averages the country's percentile rankings on ten

topics, made up of a variety of indicators and giving equal weight to each topic. Sierra Leone's position on the index reflects the severity of the institutional constraints on doing business in postwar Sierra Leone. Notably, on the ease of employing workers, Sierra Leone ranks 171 out of 175, and 168 out of 175 on the ease of registering property. Commercial laws are generally outdated. To address this problem, the government has set up the Law Reform Commission to draft new laws. The land tenure system outside of Freetown, the national capital—which generally precludes free hold—is another constraint to agricultural development (see section on rural development in this chapter).

Low levels of domestic savings and investments in Sierra Leone necessitate considerable foreign investment to support the development process. Attracting foreign investment would require improving infrastructure and the institutional environment for doing business in Sierra Leone. Sierra Leone will also have to live down the damage done to its reputation by the war. While building a good image for a country takes time, the process can be improved by advertising and other government efforts. Recent developments indicate that the country is being used as a hub for smuggling dangerous drugs to Europe. This would only serve to further damage Sierra Leone's war-ravaged image if it is not countered by swift and decisive government action.

The Rural Sector

The development of the rural economy, especially agriculture, is critical to raise living standards and provide livelihoods to abundant unemployed, unskilled labor, including former combatants. Before the war, rural households accounted for about 70 percent of Sierra Leone's population and produced the bulk of agricultural output, which accounted for over 35 percent of GDP from 1961 through 2000. However, rural households have faced major constraints: poor infrastructure, disease prevalence, underdeveloped credit and commodity markets, and explicit and implicit agricultural taxation. Unsurprisingly, agricultural productivity has been low. Rice, the staple food, accounts for well over half of the total area cropped. Yet the country has been a net rice importer since the 1950s. That Sierra Leone is also a net food importer reinforces the importance of agriculture. There is considerable scope for increasing food production. Only about 10 percent of arable land is actually under cultivation at any time. Despite abundant unemployed labor, ironically, labor shortage remains a constraint to agriculture (Food and Agriculture Organization, 2005). An issue is the rural land tenure system, which precludes freehold. Critics argue that the system serves as a disincentive for rural investment. Moreover, young rural men, who constituted the bulk of the rebel movement, often cited an unjust rural land tenure system as a motivation for joining the rebellion (Richards 2005; Peters 2006). Rural land tenure remains politically sensitive. Thus, despite its demerits and pressure from donors, reform does not appear to be on the horizon.

Integrating the rural economy into the national economy and developing rural markets will enhance commercial production. This requires the construction of feeder roads, and provision of extension services to encourage farmers to use improved methods and inputs. The government has been distributing Nerica rice seedlings, a new variety with much higher yields, to farmers. This is a good practice.

A decentralization program was initiated in 2004 to promote stronger citizen participation in economic and political governance and better service delivery. Local government institutions were abolished in 1972, leaving chiefs, the traditional leaders, with considerable unchecked powers, such as presiding over courts, administering land, and supervising public works. Such powers were often abused and have been cited by many ex-combatants as a reason for joining the rebellion (Richards 2005; Peters 2006). Elected district councils with powers to charge poll taxes and supervise service deliveries have been reestablished. Decentralization might reduce the risk of future conflict by reducing the chiefs' powers and increasing popular participation in governance. Fiscal decentralization might raise fiscal revenues and the efficiency of fiscal expenditures with the direct participation of the intended beneficiaries and local stakeholders. However, there is scope for corruption at the local level due to reduced focus and scrutiny vis-à-vis Freetown, where attention is usually focused. Corruption was reportedly a major problem in the 1960s before local councils were abolished (Fanthorpe 2006). Human resource constraints are likely to be another problem.

The Need for Economic Transformation

Economic management has tended to be short-term-oriented over the years. The prewar economic crisis left little room for long-term policymaking. Postwar, the focus has been short-to-medium term. For instance, the Poverty Reduction Strategy Paper covers a three-year period. This focus will have to change, however, as development is a long-term process that requires long-term policies. A key long-term issue is the need for industrialization. Economic development has historically involved a transformation from an agrarian economy to an industrialized economy. Sierra Leone is highly underindustrialized. The manufacturing sector has been small, accounting for, at most, 6 percent of GDP. Manufacturing is dominated by small and medium rudimentary enterprises. Without industrialization, there is limited scope for generating employment and economic growth and for raising living standards. Industrialization leads to large-scale production, which in turn requires large markets. In this regard, regional integration is essential for Sierra Leone and its neighbors, which are generally relatively small economies. Regional integration would reduce barriers to trade and provide market opportunities for accommodating the industrialization process. Sierra Leone's neighbors were instrumental in fuelling or combating the rebellion in Sierra Leone. Thus, improved security would be an added boon to regional integration.

Human resource development would be part of a long-term development strategy. Sierra Leone's literacy levels are among the lowest in Africa. Table 7.2 shows that the adult literacy rate is 35 percent in Sierra Leone, compared with 60 percent in sub-Saharan Africa. Life expectancy at birth is forty-two years, compared to fifty in sub-Saharan Africa. The provision of broad-based basic education would serve to raise general literacy levels. Although basic education is currently tuition-free in public schools, other charges, mostly unofficial, make it costly for poor people. Another major task will be to eliminate ghost teachers and schools on government payrolls, a perennial problem.

There is a need to align Sierra Leone's educational system with its development needs and priorities, and to identify and cater for skills that are likely to be in demand in the labor market. The mismatch between the country's educational output and its labor market needs has been glaring (Davies 2007). Tertiary education has been skewed toward the liberal arts, with little skills formation. Absent reliable statistics, graduate unemployment in these disciplines is known to be widespread. The low life

Table 7.2   Life expectancy and literacy in Sierra Leone and sub-Saharan Africa

	Sierra Leone	*Sub-Saharan Africa*
Adult literacy	34.8	60.3
Life expectancy at birth	41.8	49.6

Source: UNDP Human Development Report (2007–2008)

expectancy in Sierra Leone reflects the poor state of the country's health system. Greater private participation in retail health care delivery, as discussed already, is recommended.

Conclusion

Sierra Leone faces a primordial development challenge of managing a large natural resource base to alleviate widespread poverty. The civil war has added the imperative of peacebuilding to this challenge. A long-time horizon for economic management would be required to address this challenge. Issues relating to rural land tenure, institutional constraints in doing business, and human resource development will need to be addressed. The development of the rural economy, especially agriculture, will be critical in enhancing food security, raising living standards, and providing livelihoods to unemployed unskilled labor, including former combatants. While external assistance would be indispensable in the short term, efficient management of the country's natural resources would reduce aid dependence and raise domestic revenue generating capacity. Efficient management would entail enhancing Sierra Leone's capacity to negotiate favorable terms with exploiting firms, curtailing corruption, provision of basic information about the resources, and improving government's capacity to police the resources. Additional concerns for diamonds relate to their potential to undermine peace and security. The creation of alternative sources of employment to diamond mining—through rural development—would help address the problem. With regard to service delivery, widespread corruption and general inefficiencies highlight the need to discontinue the conflation in government ministries of the functions of policy management, spending, and retail service delivery. Increased privatization is recommended in retail service delivery of health and education services in order to foster competition and efficiency.

References

Abdullah, I., 1997. Bush path to destruction: The origin and character of the Revolutionary United Front. *Africa Development* 23 (3): 45–76.

Davies, Victor A. B. 2000. Sierra Leone: Ironic tragedy. *Journal of African Economies* 9 (3): 349–69.

———. 2007. Sierra Leone's economic growth performance: 1961–2000. In *The political economy of Africa: Country case studies*, ed. B. Ndulu *and others*, 660–96. *Cambridge*: Cambridge University Press.

————. 2008. Post-war capital flight and inflation. *Journal of Peace Research*, 45 (4): 519–37.

Fanthorpe. 2006. On the limits of liberal peace: Chiefs and democratic decentralization in post-war Sierra Leone. *African Affairs* 105 (418): 27–49.

Food and Agricultural Organization. 2005. Sierra Leone food aid strategy. Rome, Italy: Food and Agricultural Organization.

Government of Sierra Leone. 2007. Budget statement. Freetown: Ministry of Finance and Economic Development.

Government of Sierra Leone. 2008. Budget statement. Freetown: Ministry of Finance and Economic Development.

International Crisis Group. 2008. Sierra Leone: A new era of reform? *Africa Report* 143.

International Monetary Fund. 2006. Enhanced heavily indebted poor countries initiative: Completion point document and multilateral debt initiative. Washington, DC: International Monetary Fund.

International Monetary Fund. 2007. Sierra Leone: 2006 Article IV consultation: First review under the three-year arrangement. Washington, DC: International Monetary Fund.

Levin, E. A., and L. Gberie. 2006. Dealing for development? A story of diamond marketing and pricing in Sierra Leone. Ottawa: Diamond Development Initiative.

Moyers, R. 2003. The feasibility of establishing a formal credit delivery mechanism for small-scale diamond miners in Kono district, Sierra Leone. Report prepared for Management Systems International.

Peters, K. 2006. Footpaths to reintegration: Armed conflict, youth and the rural crisis in Sierra Leone. PhD diss., Wageningen University.

Reno, William. 1995. *Corruption and state politics in Sierra Leone*. Cambridge: Cambridge University Press.

Richards, P. 2005 To fight or to farm? Agrarian dimensions of the Mano River conflicts (Liberia and Sierra Leone). *African Affairs* 104 (417): 571–90.

United Nations Development Program. 2007. *Human development report 2007/08*. New York: Palgrave Macmillan.

United States Agency for International Development. 2001. Sierra Leone: Conflict diamonds. *Progress report on diamond policy and development programme*. USAID, Office of Transition Initiatives.

World Bank. 2009. World development indicators September 2009. *Worldbank.org*. http://econ.worldbank.org/WBSITE/EXTERNAL/EXTDEC/0,,menuPK:47682 3~pagePK:64165236~piPK:64165141~theSitePK:469372,00.html.

8

Peacebuilding and Human Security in Postwar Sierra Leone

A Critical Analysis

Earl Conteh-Morgan

Introduction

The political economy of peacebuilding in this era of extensive global-ization is often characterized by a preoccupation with maintaining the integrity of the Westphalian state and the international system on which it is built. Accordingly, there is often a discrepancy between the procedural aspects of peacebuilding and its substantive aspects. The former is mainly emphasized with a focus on state sovereignty and defense of the existing international order, with its neglect of salient issues of human security. In other words, peacebuilding is viewed as synonymous with merely putting the "state" back together, while at the same time relegating to a second-ary level the substantive and salient issues of existential insecurity: unem-ployment, lack of adequate food, healthcare, education, and the like. The consequence is that postconflict peacebuilding ends up failing to alleviate or enhance individual, group, or nationwide insecurities that were largely responsible for the outbreak of war.

This chapter is a critical discussion and evaluation of the political, psy-chocultural, and socioeconomic dimensions of peacebuilding efforts in Sierra Leone since the signing of the July 1999 Lomé Peace Accord and the end of hostilities in 2002 to the present. In other words, how substantive has postwar peacebuilding been from 2002 to the present? What has been the impact of peacebuilding on human security in Sierra Leone? On a comparative basis, has the entire process of peacebuilding been more heavily state-centric than people-centered? Is real emancipation from intolerable inequalities taking place in Sierra Leone? This discussion and evaluation will revolve around the examination of such questions.

Peacebuilding efforts, whether in Africa or other developing regions, are still heavily influenced by traditional conceptions of security. That is why in current postconflict peacebuilding efforts, state insecurity is viewed as synonymous with an attack on the integrity of the state (Abiew and Keating 2000). As a result of this state-centric view of peacebuilding, many postconflict societies have been unable to alleviate many of the existential insecurities that led to civil strife. What often happens is that traditional conceptions of national security intrude in the process of peacebuilding, whereby people are viewed as the "means" to political stability as opposed to being the "end" of all peacebuilding efforts. People are also viewed as the means to a stable state, conducive to the infiltration and enhancement of globalization trends. In the end, human security, broadly defined, is subverted or marginalized.

Conceptual Clarifications: Peacebuilding, Human Security

Peacebuilding, with a view toward attaining long-term peace, involves transforming the social and political environment that fosters intolerable inequality, engenders historical grievances, and nurtures adversarial interactions. This means developing the political will that promotes social, political, and economic infrastructures that produce tolerable inequality, and prevent future violence. The focus is on dismantling structures that contribute to violent conflict, in particular, moving beyond short-term functions of maintaining a cease-fire, demobilization and disarmament, and monitoring competitive elections among former adversaries.

Human Security is a situation or condition that guarantees freedom from fear and need at the personal, community, or group, and national levels. It also involves psychocultural, socioeconomic, and political well being that contributes to sustainable or durable peace. Attaining such a pervasive view of human security involves an understanding of the underlying structure of privilege and marginalization, along with political will and economic power to deal with them so they contribute to sustainable peace. A willingness to understand human insecurities (economic, health, food, etc.) in terms of those who experience them is a necessary condition for success.

The Lomé Accord

The conflict that plagued Sierra Leone between 1991 and 2001 resulted in the collapse of social and economic structures. Infrastructure was damaged and educational and health services deteriorated even further, not to mention the psychological trauma generated by the intensity and duration of the violence within all parts of the country. Overall, development has been severely undermined as a result of physical, human, and psychological damage associated with the war. However, the underlying causes of war in Sierra Leone may have been marginalized in favor of peace between the government and the Revolutionary United Front (RUF). The primary causes of conflict in the country were, in particular, marginalization and exclusion of many groups from economic and political opportunities (Hirsch 2001; Gberie 2005). Moreover, a formidable and often overlooked cause of Sierra Leone's civil conflict is the external one—the new political economy of neoliberalism—with its emphasis on a sudden reintroduction of multiparty politics—and structural adjustment policies. These accelerated the intense economic deprivation and existential insecurities resulting in the emergence of the RUF and its incredible brutality.

At the height of the war, and when the core of the Sierra Leone state (Freetown) was itself under siege in 1999, the peace accords became more effective, driven by external imperatives. Prior to the Lomé Peace Accord of July 1999, earlier peacemaking initiatives aimed at a negotiated settlement of the conflict culminated in the Abidjan Peace Accord of November 30, 1996, and the ECOWAS Peace Plan of October 23, 1997. However, peace accords are often very successful in putting together a government, setting dates for elections, and spelling out specifics about power sharing between the parties in conflict. For instance, in the Lomé accord, chairmanship of the board of the Commission for the Management of Strategic Resources, National Reconstruction and Development (CMRRD) was offered to the leader of the RUF, Corporal Foday Sankoh. He was also offered the vice presidency, answerable only to the president of Sierra Leone. The government of Sierra Leone was also mandated to give ministerial positions to the RUF, especially in one of the senior cabinet appointments of finance, foreign affairs, and justice, as well as other cabinet positions (Lomé Peace Accord 1999). The RUF was also not barred from holding senior government positions. To a large extent, the Lomé accord is an externally driven treaty whose objective was to ensure the sovereignty of the Sierra Leone state, with little or no emphasis on alleviating the insecurities of individuals and groups.

In particular, the Lomé accord did not underscore the need for a just peace, since Article IX even mandated the Sierra Leone government to "take appropriate legal steps to grant Corporal Foday Sankoh absolute and free pardon" (Lomé Peace Accord 1999, Article IX). In light of the mass killings, rapes, and terrible atrocities the RUF had committed up to that point, the accord and this specific provision constituted an affront and generated an outrage to many. As in many peace accords, the disproportionate emphasis is always on "state integrity" or ensuring "negative peace"—a condition of nonviolence in the midst of continued corruption, blatant inequities, and dysfunctional institutions that contribute to disabilities and even death. For instance, Article XIII of the Lomé accord mandates the Economic Community of West African States Monitoring Group (ECOMOG) to engage in peacekeeping that would ensure the security of the state of Sierra Leone. The immediate motivation of the accord was the RUF invasion of Freetown (the seat of government), which was viewed by the international community as the near total collapse of the Sierra Leone state. Accordingly, international pressure was brought to bear on both rebels and the Kabbah government to negotiate a settlement to the conflict.

The Lomé accord in particular, as well as the entire peacebuilding process in Sierra Leone, underscores the procedural aspects of peacebuilding, such as peacekeeping—monitoring cease-fire violations—ensuring demobilizations, focusing on humanitarian relief that is often short-term, or a special fund for war victims that is also short-term in its impact and is often a part of international humanitarian relief.

The Political State-centric Focus

Peacebuilding efforts in Sierra Leone since the official end of the war in 2002 involved many actors at the international, regional, and national levels. The war greatly undermined authority, age-old traditional attitudes, and professionalism. One consequence in particular was blatant disregard for community values such that individuals and groups were forced to take violent action against people or organizations believed to be agents of insecurity (Sierra-leone.org 1999). The task of peacebuilding, with a view toward long-term peace, would focus on eliminating the mind-set that compelled people to distrust and question their sociopolitical and psychological environment. This translates into efforts toward eliminating structural and cultural sources of insecurity or a process of resocialization in order to strengthen commonly held traditional ideas and understandings of political and social life. However, in Sierra Leone, again, there was more emphasis placed on the procedural aspects of ensuring the integrity of the state than there was on the substantive aspects of ensuring a sustainable and long-term peace. For instance, in Sierra Leone, the National Committee for

Such as peacekeeping

Disarmament, Demobilization and Reintegration (NCDDR), aided by the United Nations Mission in Sierra Leone (UNAMSIL), quickly disarmed close to eighty thousand fighters in less than two years (UNAMSIL 2006a, 2006b). This accomplishment meant that the state's sovereignty and overall governmental control of national security was again restored in the country. Even within the NCDDR framework, not much has been accomplished in the area of reintegration. According to many observers, after the demilitarization and demobilization, there was very little, or no, money available for the reintegration process of peacebuilding. Reintegration is often more involved, complex, and requires a greater expenditure of resources because of (1) the need to train ex-combatants in skills that would help them secure gainful employment; (2) the need to reconstruct the national economy with a long-term view toward decreasing unemployment levels nationwide; and (3) the overall and necessary goal of promoting reconciliation and a just peace.

In Sierra Leone, however, peacebuilding has been viewed as a short-term activity with a disproportionate focus on demilitarization and demobilization as the end goal. In other words, the top-level external actors, like the UN and powerful international donors, often conceive of peacebuilding as ensuring the state's integrity or sovereignty while deemphasizing all the structural violence factors that contributed to secondary violence of community and national destruction. Even after the massive disarming of hundreds of thousands of combatants and the restoration of state authority, Zinurine Alghali (2007, 24) observed the following: "There remain numerous challenges to sustainable post-conflict reintegration in Sierra Leone. Only about 54,439 ex-combatants benefited from the skills training program, whilst only about 45,000 ex-combatants (as well as some dependents) received food and cooking utensils. Even the fortunate ones who did receive training found it extremely difficult to secure employment due to unavailability of jobs."

Alghali's observation underscores the fact that in postwar societies, the primary difficulty encountered in peacebuilding is often in the area of economic reintegration of not just ex-combatants, but of all economically deprived citizens.

Sierra Leone may have fallen short of pursuing a peacebuilding agenda with a view toward alleviating human insecurity. Such an agenda involves transforming the socioeconomic and political environment that fosters tolerable inequality, eliminates historical grievances, and discourages adversarial interactions. This may mean the development of social, political, and economic infrastructures that produce distributional justice and prevent future violence. The focus is on dismantling structures that contribute to conflict, in particular moving beyond short-term functions of peacebuilding.

The lack of resources for engaging in the long-term reintegration functions of job creation, skills training, and community integration has resulted in continuing joblessness, many without skills training, lingering resentment against ex-combatants in local communities, and lack of opportunities in general for women and ex-combatants.

While peacebuilding is supposed to be holistic, involving security, socioeconomics, human rights, reconciliation, and resource mobilization, among other factors, it is especially education and employment that are central to a stable and long-term peace (Murithi 2006). For example, in Sierra Leone, the youth (aged 18–35) bulge was particularly responsible for much of the violence. While many were forcibly recruited to fight in the war, they were also a segment of the nation with high expectations for gainful employment and the hope that they would be provided with the skills necessary to effectively reintegrate into a postwar Sierra Leone. The youth of Sierra Leone are especially significant to the success of peacebuilding because they constitute more than 50 percent of the nation's population. Both youth ex-combatants and the rest of the youth population have not been provided with skills relevant for individual and national development. Many of these youths had joined in the fighting as a way to compensate for their lack of self-esteem, caused by their lack of education and employment. Their continued lack of education, skills, and employment could have a destabilizing effect in the long run, or may even contribute to an increase in criminal activities in the country.

The problem of effective youth integration into societal opportunities and provision of avenues for individual self-actualization constitute a major, if not the most significant, failure in Sierra Leone's peacebuilding process. The conflict in Sierra Leone, its intensity, and the level of participation in it by youths could be explained in terms of how their identities, ideas, and goals were affected. The socially constructed (Searle 1995; Finnemore and Sikkink 2001) understanding and the perceptions or interpretations of the youth shape the way in which peacebuilding cooperation or reconciliation could unfold. For instance, it could be argued that youth rebels' understanding of who they are—whether in Sierra Leone, Liberia, or the Democratic Republic of Congo—as well as what they consider legitimate and want to achieve, had their origins in their social environment, an environment characterized by injustice, gross inequalities, and oppression. In other words, the social relationships (exploitation, corruption, and the like) in which groups (youth, women, individuals, etc.) find themselves determine how they interpret events and others' actions, how they define interests, and how they pursue goals, whether peacefully or through the use of violence.

The Psychosocial Dimensions of Peacebuilding

Both material and ideational (norms, values, mores, etc.) factors are deeply interconnected (Onuf 1989; Ruggie 1998). However, where peacebuilding efforts overemphasize the political (with its power-centered focus) at the expense of the normative integrity of individuals, groups, and communities, these efforts may not contribute to long-term peace in a society in need of holistic security. Since the widely shared intersubjective beliefs (especially deep-seated psychological and moral values) in a war-torn country are often destroyed by violence and intercommunal bloodletting, the purpose of reintegration and rehabilitation should be, for instance, to collectively reemphasize held ideas of mutual support and sharing, the centrality of the extended family, respect for elders, recognition of customs and taboos, among other factors, especially in a postwar society with a large traditional and rural sector like Sierra Leone (Wessells 1997). However, in Sierra Leone, the very necessary aspects of peacebuilding—including trauma healing and psychological counseling, civic education, and extensive sensitization of local communities—were either poorly implemented or lacking. Sierra Leone in particular did not institute or utilize local or traditional methods of peacebuilding, as in Rwanda, as a way of strengthening or further democratizing, through widespread participation, the process of reconciliation and education of local communities (Barnes and Polzer 2000).

Judging from the many challenges peacebuilding efforts face in postconflict societies in the world, it can be said that traditional Westphalian conceptions of peacebuilding have to be reconsidered or complemented if a self-sustaining peace is to become a reality in a country like Sierra Leone. There is, in other words, a need for new concepts and practices that can advance the ideals of a positive peace (Galtung 1969). For Sierra Leone, self-sustaining peace not only means the cessation of hostilities, which has already been achieved, but also the strengthening and reassertion of normative structures that enable individuals and groups to share common identities, understandings, and expectations that enhance a social order that eliminates corruption and alleviates all forms of existential insecurity. Traditional or modern conceptions of peacebuilding largely promote negative peace by emphasizing state-security and state-building mechanisms to the near neglect of basic human needs. Examples, however, show that this approach often does not translate into self-sustaining peace in places like Liberia after its first war, Afghanistan, or most of the former Yugoslavia.

To a large extent, reconciliatory mechanisms are the domain of ideas, norms, and identities. For example, in Sierra Leone, the effort toward political reintegration and social rehabilitation could be hampered by strong feelings of hatred, mistrust, and fear among groups in society. In discussions with ordinary Sierra Leoneans, for example, it is easy to see the high level of contempt for people in uniform, especially soldiers because of their connivance with the RUF, notorious for its heinous crimes (Conteh-Morgan and Dixon-Fyle 1999). Among ordinary people, there is still a high level of mistrust of police, soldiers, ex-civil defense force members, and government officials. Because of the prevailing high levels of social distance in many postconflict societies, a key objective of peacebuilding is to foster a dimension of human security that nurtures a culture based on tolerance, cooperation, and empathy. It involves a deliberate effort to deconstruct the negative images of the "other" that prevailed during the years of conflict. Often, the pervasive violence of civil conflict does not totally destroy the discourses, ideas, and institutions that communities shared and collectively upheld during the years of peace. In Sierra Leone, these are "social facts" such as the extended family, village solidarity, respect for elders, or the sanctity of human life, among others, which serve as the bedrock of national reconciliation. The problem with state-centered peacebuilding is that it is often characterized by internationally backed mechanisms, structures, and ideas that lack indigenous legitimacy since these factors are not products of internal, intersubjective understandings or agreements. For example, because the 1999 American-sponsored Lomé Peace Accord was largely externally imposed, it was not surprising that fighting broke out again in May 2000. The accord was focused solely on making peace between the government and RUF, such that amnesty was granted to all, and about 2,230 fighters from different rival groups were absorbed, unscreened, into the new army (Dowden 2002). In other words, wholly state-centric or externally imposed peacebuilding measures do not encourage postwar communities to critically reflect on their own sociopolitical and economic conditions so that they can determine, as well as substantially contribute to, the development of mechanisms of peaceful change best suited for their society.

Moreover, in order to underscore the significance of psychosocial healing and social reintegration, it is worthwhile to examine whether traditional methods of conflict resolution, such as the *barrae* (barray) system, were extensively utilized. Were these methods only used to complement the work of the Truth and Reconciliation Commission? Sierra Leone has traditionally had a very strong system of local conflict resolution (barrae), particularly among the Temne and Mende. Perhaps an extensive and effective use of this system could have enhanced the peacebuilding process and effectively ensured an end to a culture of impunity. The barrae system has both reconciliatory and punitive dimensions because of the full participation by elders and the common people in community conflict resolution.

The extensive use of the barrae system, with minimal interference by the government or the external world, would have been ideal for Sierra Leone since there were so many participants (the Sierra Leone Army, the various civil defense forces, the RUF, etc.) in the war. This means the entire Sierra Leone society needs healing, especially at the very local levels. An extensive and effective, as well as autonomous, use of the barrae system would help resuscitate that cultural dimension of Sierra Leone society and would later contribute to law and order in local communities. Moreover, decentralization of power is enhanced when traditional cultural resources are encouraged to operate fully and effectively. The central government is then free to deal with more overarching problems of governance, while local political and cultural systems deal with the more community-specific issues of the nation as a whole.

Global governability + R2P

Economic Liberalization and Human Insecurity

Often, for example, in the case of African states, there is an inherent tension between external impositions (e.g., neoliberal internationalism) and communal African lifestyles. Thus, an African model of human security, especially with regard to human rights, broadly defined, may be more relevant for sustainable peacebuilding and human security. Josiah Cobbah (1987), in his critique of the Western rights tradition, captures the relevance of the African model of human rights for peace stability and security. He emphasizes communalism, duties and hierarchy: "Within the organization of African social life one can discern various organizing principles. As a people, Africans emphasize groupings, sameness, and commonality. Rather than the survival of the fittest and control over nature, the African worldview is tempered with the general guiding principle of the survival of the entire community and a sense of cooperation, interdependence and collective responsibility . . . Although African society is communal, it is [also] hierarchical." Since universal human rights emphasize a Lockean abstraction of natural rights, certain groups (women, minorities in general) have not fared well because the Western-rights tradition assumes an abstract equality of all individuals, and downplays the reality of discrimination based on group identity, which undermines individual, group, and human security in general. Especially in a non-Western postconflict society, the relevance of culture is significant for protecting the rights of the less powerful.

Cobbah's (1987) critique is especially very significant for Sierra Leone when applied to neoliberalism and its emphasis on trade and open markets. If Sierra Leone continues to operate on the assumed economic efficiency of neoliberal economic philosophy, it does not necessarily mean

distributional justice would be guaranteed. Sierra Leone's woes, in the first place, were precipitated by the severe lack of distributional justice embedded in IMF and World Bank austerity measures (Weeks 1992). Many view the ongoing, or completed, peacebuilding process as still lacking in the area of economic security because of the negative effects of the structural adjustment policies. These policies end up undermining, rather than enhancing, peacebuilding, especially in the areas of employment and overall economic security. The new political economy of neoliberal economics was a severe shock to many fragile states like Sierra Leone that have not quite recovered, even after they imploded and are undergoing postwar reconstruction.

Instead of requiring Sierra Leone and similar war-torn societies to immediately adopt austerity measures or open markets, these societies should instead be allowed to introduce these measures in piecemeal fashion until their economies are strong enough to compete within the neoliberal international system. Sierra Leone, for example, should be aided not only to find more markets for its raw materials, but it should also be allowed to reintroduce subsidies in critical areas like food and health, as well as tariffs that would encourage its farmers to want to produce even more commodities.

A gradual implementation of the new ideology of globalization in Sierra Leone would temper the negative effects of social transformation in the early twenty-first century. The rapid pace of globalization and westernization are both seriously eroding the respect of the youth for the elders and traditional hierarchies of authority that are necessary for maintaining the hegemony of indigenous approaches to peacebuilding. Communalism and the primacy of elders in maintaining traditional ceremonies are rapidly giving way to individualism and private accumulation. As a result of their incorporation into the market economy and commercialization, many traditional societies are in a state of transition. The consequences are that communal societies are experiencing serious challenges to their societal structure, security, survival, and traditional moral foundations. Because traditional moral foundations are disintegrating, warfare has become vicious and waged with more sophisticated firearms, with little or no regard for women, children, or the elderly.

Conclusions

A very effective and long lasting peace in Sierra Leone would mean the utilization of both modern (Westphalian) and revitalized indigenous institutions of governance. One major reason for the Sierra Leone war was the urban bias of rural-urban disparity in allocating the resources of development. In Sierra Leone, since the official socialization process has been so Western-oriented, there should be very conscious and deliberate steps taken to relegitimize indigenous institutions and mechanisms that would directly cater to the psychological needs of the majority of rural people. In other words, a more direct participant democratic environment is necessary for sustained peace at the national level. Many decisions made at the central-government level in the capital city have been like fiats directed at the rural people. Such decisions are, therefore, not seen as legitimate because they may not address local problems.

Traditional indigenous societies, by their very nature, tend to be communal, collective, and more prone to fostering an atmosphere of peaceful coexistence. The application of traditional customs and values in reconciliation efforts may result in more communal grassroots involvement, thereby substantially contributing to eradication of the root causes of the conflict and to holistic peacebuilding. Within this context, culture is viewed as the primary explanation of change; it is, by nature, intersubjective, and has real constitutive force. Traditional cultures are often characterized by methods embedded in ethnic wisdom for effectively resolving conflicts. However, the influence of westernization and external impositions may lead to their demise.

In particular, the peacebuilding process, if it is to alleviate a great deal of the existential insecurity in Sierra Leone, should aim at the following steps: (1) job security or increased employment levels for youth (18–35 years); (2) health security for the general population, and in particular deal with postwar traumatic stress for ex-combatants; (3) community security, by dealing with the rise in criminal activities; and (4) food security related to the global rise in food shortage, among other things. This means that effective international assistance, either from the UN or other external actors, involves understanding the cognitive structures of those who have experienced war-related violence and trauma and providing the appropriate peacebuilding activities to assist them. Together, members of the postwar society invent the properties of the new society. Reality cannot be imposed from outside or by the powerful, and such reality does not exist prior to its social (collective) invention. Moreover, the knowledge that is integral to a new Sierra Leone should be socially and culturally constructed. In the final analysis, a blend of modern and traditional methods of peacebuilding should be ongoing. In some countries, the blend would be effective; in others, depending on the time and other various factors, it might not. It would be worthwhile for local NGOs to encourage the process of blending the external and the indigenous in order to ensure a more holistic approach toward peacebuilding and human security.

References

Abiew, Francis Kofi, and Tom Keating. 2000. Outside agents and the politics of peacebuilding and reconciliation. *International Journal* 4 (1): 15–31.

Alghali, Zinurine A. 2007. Post-conflict reintegration challenges in Sierra Leone. *Conflict Ttrends: ACCORD* 1:16–21.

Barnes, Catherine, and Tara Polzer. 2000. Sierra Leone peace process: Learning from the past to address current challenges. http://www.c-r.org/resources/occasional -papers/occasional-papers-archive.php.

Cobbah, Josiah A. M. 1987. African values and the human rights debate: An African perspective. *Human Rights Quarterly* 9 (3): 307–21.

Conteh-Morgan, Earl, and Mac Dixon-Fyle. 1999. *Sierra Leone at the end of the twentieth century: History, politics, and society.* New York: Peter Lang.

Dowden, Richard. 2002. Justice goes on trial in Sierra Leone. *The Guardian,* October 3.

Finnemore, Martha, and Kathryn Sikkink. 2001. Taking stock: The Constructivist Research Program in International Relations and Comparative Politics. *Annual Review of Political Science* 4: 391–416.

Gberie, Lansana. 2001. *A dirty war in West Africa: The RUF and the destruction of Sierra Leone.* Bloomington: Indiana University Press.

Hirsch, John L. 2001. Sierra Leone: Diamonds and the struggle for democracy. Boulder, CO: Lynne Rienner.

Lomé Peace Accord. 1999. Peace agreement between the government of Sierra Leone and the Revolutionary United Front of Sierra Leone. http://www.sierra -leone.org/lomeaccord.html.

Murithi, Tim. 2006. The AU/NEPAD post conflict reconstruction policy: An analysis. *Conflict Trends: ACCORD* 1:16–21.

Onuf, N. 1989. *Worlds of our making.* Columbia: University of South Carolina Press.

Ruggie, John G. 1998. *Constructing the world polity: Essays on international institutionalization.* London: Routledge.

Searle, John R. 1995. *The construction of social reality.* New York: Free Press.

Sierra-leone.org. 1999b. News archive. http://www.sierra-leone.org/slnews.html.

United Nations Mission in Sierra Leone. 2006a. Demobilization, demilitarization, and reintegration (DDR) coordination section. http://www.un.org./en/ peacekeeping/missions/past/unamsil/UnamsilRS.htm.

———. 2006b. National committee for disarmament, demobilization, and reintegration. http://www.un.org/en/peacekeeping/missions/past/Unamsil/ Overview/pdf

Weeks, John. 1992. *Development strategy and the economy of Sierra Leone.* New York: Palgrave Macmillan.

Wessells, Mike. 1997. Child soldiers. *Bulletin of Atomic Scientists,* November–December. http://pangaea.org/street_children/africa/armies.htm.

9

Global Inequalities and Peace in Postwar Sierra Leone

Marda Mustapha

Introduction

Scholars have argued, from various angles, that the interaction of bad governance, global economic shocks, the exacting demands of structural adjustment, and the deleterious impacts of implementing such policies on the population of Sierra Leone since the 1980s led to the outbreak of the ten-year civil war from 1991 through 2001 (Richards 1996; Abdullah 1998; Kandeh 1999; Zack-Williams 1999; Chege 2002; Rashid 2004; Riddell 2005; Grant 2005; Keen 2005). Since the Lomé Peace Accord of 2000, Sierra Leone has been in a state of negative peace—a situation characterized by the absence of direct violence (Ramsbotham, Woodhouse, and Miall 2005)—having failed thus far to put in place the conditions for sustainable, positive peace. Studies on the challenges of achieving positive peace in postwar nations like Sierra Leone have focused almost exclusively on the internal dynamics of structural violence[1] (Lamin 2003; MacIntyre and Thusi 2003; Conteh-Morgan 2004; Rippon and Willow 2004). Such studies have neglected, to a large extent, the broader impacts of global capitalism—and its attendant forms of inequality—that is reflected in these internal dynamics that perpetuate structural violence and frustrate the achievement of positive peace.

Sierra Leone is listed at the bottom of the United Nations Development Program's (UNDP) human development index (UNDP 2009). The International Monetary Fund (IMF) report (2005) highlights the pervasiveness of poverty in Sierra Leone, where about 75 percent of the population subsists on less than US$2 a day. Youth unemployment and disaffection, rampant corruption (both real and perceived), and infant mortality are all on the increase; the health sector struggles to cope with rising demand; and the educational system lacks adequate funding. The persistence of these conditions has led to worries that Sierra Leone could relapse into renewed conflict. While such factors can be useful indicators of the potential for a recurrence of direct violence, it is perhaps even more important for scholars to broaden the scope of analyses beyond these internal dynamics to include consideration of how structural violence is shaped and exacerbated by the dynamics of global political economy.

This chapter argues that the persistence of structural violence, a major obstacle to the attainment of positive peace in Sierra Leone, reflects larger global inequalities produced by neoliberal regimes to service world capitalism's needs. The reproduction or reflection of global inequalities in postwar nations like Sierra Leone are made possible through a series of policy socializations by international financial institutions (IFI) such as the World Bank and the IMF. In addition, the socioeconomic strains brought about by the neoliberal policies of the IFIs have facilitated the politicization of the state, clientelism, and neopatrimonialism in postwar Sierra Leone. Therefore, the entrenched structure of global capitalist political economy, held in place by those who both direct and gain most from its workings, suggests that Sierra Leone will be increasingly less, rather than more, likely to effectively deal with its own internal structural violence and its resultant inequalities. To minimize structural violence and achieve positive peace, postwar and third world countries like Sierra Leone should be given meaningful agency and participation in decisions that structure the global political economy, especially when such countries are struggling to achieve positive peace.

Global Inequalities

Proponents of globalization dismiss or dispute claims that growing conditions of abject poverty and the growing global inequality are byproducts of globalization and capitalism, instead attributing them to "imprudent national policies" tainted by graft and political corruption (Gilpin 2001). A growing body of research in recent years, however, suggests that rapid integration of the world's poorest countries into the global capitalist economy (GCE) since the 1970s (Murshed 2005) subjected them to radically unequal terms of competition with the wealthy and advanced economies of the north, who dictate GCE rules of engagement. The vastly disproportionate benefits derived by industrialized nations vis-à-vis poorer nations

WS T

like Sierra Leone in the GCE have been widely documented by scholars and international aid agencies like Oxfam and Human Rights Watch, as well as by the United Nation's annual reports. Evidence of the negative impacts of global economic convergence include the ever-widening gap between rich and poor, both among and within nations, widespread exploitation of unprotected workers, "environmental degradation . . . and devastation of national economies" wrought by "unregulated international financial flows" (Gilpin 2001, 9).

These conditions are some of the principal hallmarks of both structural violence and global inequality illustrative of the impacts of policies shaped at the global level on the local political economies of poor nations like Sierra Leone. Recent studies suggest that global capitalism has also contributed significantly to the outbreak of violent civil conflicts over the past three decades (Zack-Williams 1999; Murshed 2005), correlating economic disparities at the global level with growing disparities in distribution and rising social tensions at the local level. If, as Gilpin (2001) has suggested, the endemic "structural violence" that culminates in civil war in impoverished nations like Sierra Leone is the product of "imprudent national policies," then one must ask to what degree such "imprudent policies" are themselves creatures of globalization?

The end of the cold war hastened the movement toward "a single capitalist world-economy" (Wallerstein 1998, 281). The poorest countries were drawn into global market structures as both active participants and sometimes-reluctant subscribers to a neoliberal agenda of debt restructuring policies. Susan Strange (1983) contends that the industrialized nation-states of the "north" control GCE market flows and policies through an interrelated network of international regimes, or "structural power" agencies, like the IMF, World Bank, and, more recently, state-sponsored NGOs like USAID, the German GTZ, and the British Department for International Development (DFID).

Rather than neutral agencies, international regimes structure global political economy, trade rules, debt reorganization, and other monetary issues in ways that mirror the interests of wealthy nations of the north while adversely affecting the economic welfare, national security, and political autonomy of impoverished smaller states like Sierra Leone. Through international regimes, powerful countries like the United States dictate both the "rules" and outcomes of the global economy, crafting them along lines favorable to their interests. Poor nations subscribe to these regimes while wholly lacking control over the policies and monetary decisions they make. Through international regimes, wealthy industrialized countries have succeeded in creating virtual monopolies under the guise of free trade over the world's markets, which serve as outlets for their own industrial products as well as sources of cheap labor and raw commodities (Stiglitz 2003). The World Trade Organization (WTO) is one such institution that creates and enforces international trade regimes.

WTO membership neither guarantees fair trade nor addresses disparities at global or local levels of political economy (Polaski 2006). Internally, socioeconomic gaps are widened as a result of weakened capacity for economic growth and diversification, exacerbating inequalities and diminishing the efficacy of national institutions to deal with rising structural violence within poorer countries like Sierra Leone, which pay about two-thirds of the tariffs collected in rich industrialized countries (UNDP 2005, 127). In addition, rich industrialized countries not only deny poor countries access to their agricultural markets through nontariff barriers, but they also provide their own farmers subsidies that exceed the entire GDP of sub-Saharan Africa and that are also six times higher than all foreign aid from rich countries (Goldin and Reinert 2006, 11). Subsidized commodities from wealthy nations are "dumped" in global markets at greatly reduced prices, making it difficult for smaller farmers from the world's poorest countries, like Sierra Leone, to profitably compete.

International finance intensifies global inequalities among states while also reproducing the effects of such inequality within poor countries like Sierra Leone. The governance of international finance is reserved for groupings like the G7 summit, the Basil Committee on Banking Supervision, and the Financial Stability Forum (FSF), on the one hand, and the more inclusive International Monetary Fund (IMF), on the other. The exclusive groupings only allow rich, industrialized countries to take part in the negotiations. Although the IMF allows input from poor nations, it is as heavily influenced by powerful capitalist countries as the exclusive groupings (Stiglitz 2003; Dreher and Jensen 2007). One example is the unilateral decision by the United States, with the acquiescence of the IMF, to switch from a fixed-currency exchange to a flexible rate. This change in global monetary policy clearly worked to the advantage of the United States, while it destabilized the economies of poor countries like Sierra Leone.

The monopoly held by wealthy nations over global financial governance, and their tendency to shape policies that disregard the domestic economic fundamentals of poorer states, leaves countries like Sierra Leone vulnerable and twice as likely to suffer from financial crisis sparked by upsets and downtowns at the level of GCE (American Political Science Association [APSA] 2008, 26). Indeed, poor countries like Sierra Leone have experienced greater financial volatility during phases of consumption boom (Prasad and others 2004) and bust. International institutions like the IMF and World Bank facilitated the consumption boom in poor countries like Sierra Leone through liberalization reforms that targeted the financial sector. Austere microeconomic policies were enacted, under pressure from the IMF, that required poor countries like Sierra Leone to borrow in "hard" foreign currencies, transferring the risks of exchange-rate volatility from rich industrialized countries to the poorer countries. These reforms exacerbated financial volatility, destabilized markets, and eventually sent the national economy of countries like Sierra Leone into freefall (Zack-Williams 1999).

Global trends indicate that the widening gap in global inequality will continue apace (APSA 2008). The inequality in terms of per capita income between the United States and Sierra Leone, the world's poorest country, has grown from 38.5 to 1 in 1960 to 64 to 1 in 2005 (APSA 2008, 2). Such inequality enhances the ability of rich and powerful nations or actors to impose their worldviews, institutions, and policies in the global arena, hindering the progress of poor and powerless nations like Sierra Leone (APSA 2008, 8). Global inequalities also create global social differences among countries, inhibiting the efforts of poor countries to achieve social equity, domestic peace, and economic security. Social differences are often ranked in hierarchical order such that they are associated with inequalities of power, emanating from policies and institutions that reproduce marginalization, discrimination, and even violent conflict. Global hierarchies of inequality seem to have largely shaped the political and economic institutions and social outcomes that have led to the reproduction and increase of inequalities in countries like Sierra Leone.

Reproducing Global Inequalities in Sierra Leone

Through processes of convergence, globalization has contributed to global inequalities between nations and the widening inequalities of income and opportunity within nations. International regimes shape global economic policies at the macro level, and, in doing so, exercise powerful influence over the internal political economy of countries like Sierra Leone, positioning social groups and actors in ways that mirror the broader inequalities shaped by the global capitalist economy. Therefore, to fully understand the internal dynamics (political or economic) of postwar Sierra Leone, the country must be situated within "this world economy which is to the advantage or disadvantage of particular groups located within" the country (Wallerstein 1998, 281).

Disparities of wealth and power are mutually constituted through interactions between unequal players at the level of the global economy and, at the same time, are replicated in the national socioeconomic context, making economic and political inequality an important aspect in determining whether domestic politics will promote development or stagnation (APSA 2008). In essence, global inequalities influence the persistence of structural violence through various mechanisms, including, but not limited to, the socialization of unfettered economic liberalization policies. The undue advantage enjoyed by powerful nations makes it difficult for postwar Sierra Leone to compete in the global market or to access international finance needed for development projects. The quest to access funds for development attracts stringent neoliberal macroeconomic policies dictated by the IMF and the World Bank. These policies have resulted in Sierra Leone reducing social spending and abandoning redistributive policies meant to benefit the poorest in the society. As a result, the poor suffer disproportionately from the resulting "unemployment, declining wages and reduction in social welfare programs" (APSA 2008, 35), thereby reproducing the global income inequality within Sierra Leone.

Efforts at laying the foundations for positive peace in Sierra Leone began in the immediate aftermath of the war. The government of Sierra Leone, led by Ahmed Tejan-Kabbah, carried out a relatively successful reconstruction effort targeting provincial infrastructure that had been looted and destroyed, with special attention given to education and health care facilities. The infrastructural reconstruction projects included junior secondary schools in all chiefdoms, senior secondary schools in major towns, and the rehabilitation of existing hospitals and health clinics and the building of new ones. Between 2000 and 2005, the number of schools increased rapidly to about 4,578, an increase of over 1,000 from 1996 (Wang 2007, 67). Similarly, by 2003, the government had rebuilt, refurbished, or built 927 hospitals and health centers, thereby increasing the number of health facilities by 410 percent from its war years and 19 percent from its prewar years (IAHM 2005; Statistics Sierra Leone 2008). The focus on building schools, health centers, and hospitals was partly in accordance with the larger spirit of Article XXXI of the Lomé Peace Accord, which pledged government provision of "free compulsory education for the first nine years of schooling (Basic Education)," later to be extended an additional three years. This article in the Lomé accord also bound the government to developing provisions for primary health care throughout the country. While government provided some form of free education in elementary school (six years), for example, students are expected to fund their secondary education. Furthermore, education is not compulsory, and higher education remains a privilege since post-secondary education is beyond the reach of the vast majority of Sierra Leoneans. Health care is also unaffordable, as half of the population lacks access to health services altogether because it is either too expensive or too far away.

Technological change and proliferation of nongovernmental organizations (NGOs) in postwar Sierra Leone have increased demands for skilled labor, especially that which requires computer literacy, a situation the present educational system seems to be ill-equipped to remedy. Given the austerity measures adopted by the government, their devastating effects on the provision of quality and affordable education, and the lack of technical resources to train skilled workers in these areas, Sierra Leone cannot draw on its domestic pool of labor to fill such "technically" challenging jobs in ways that would stimulate other areas of the economy and employment. Many graduates therefore find they are unemployable because of their inability to use computers. The few who are computer literate get the jobs, thereby creating an earnings gap not only between their peers, but also between them and the unskilled, thereby increasing the existing inequalities. In addition, the inability to use contemporary technology by the majority in the labor force has added to unemployment, particularly among youth and women.

Infrastructure and services such as good roads and adequate supplies of electricity are abysmally lacking. While the government of Sierra Leone rebuilt schools, hospitals, and health centers in many areas between 2000 and 2007, successive governments have been unable to provide essential services to other parts of the country. Virtually, the entire country remains without electricity, with the exception of Bo Town, Kenema Town, and an intermittent electricity supply in Freetown. The same can be said for clean drinking water, which is nonprocurable in most parts of the country. In addition, health care continues to deteriorate, and maternal mortality is the highest in the world (Amnesty International 2009; *Washington Post* 2008). The failure on the part of the government to provide these services has been attributed almost exclusively to corruption. While it is true that most people perceived the previous SLPP government as corrupt, the phenomenon and understanding of public goods is more complex than just government corruption.

The provision of public goods in Sierra Leone is mostly tied to World Bank funding based on loans almost always accompanied by interest rates, conditions, and bureaucratic protocols that sometimes considerably slow the process of its disbursement and subsequent implementation of the infrastructural project for which it was meant. Most, if not all, of the funds allocated to Sierra Leone for the rebuilding of health and educational infrastructure were in the form of grants. It is therefore not surprising that the government of Sierra Leone was able to rehabilitate damaged schools and hospitals and build additional new ones within five years following the effective end of hostilities in 2002. On the contrary, infrastructural developments not funded by grants take a lot longer to negotiate and implement. In some cases, loan negotiations, approval, and disbursements may take up to three years or more to complete. In addition, the protocol of awarding contracts for the implementation of these infrastructural projects could take another year or two. In essence, the duration of loan negotiations and the initial implementation stage of projects could take anywhere between three to five years. It is therefore not surprising that the former SLPP government could not start the infrastructural projects for which loans had been negotiated. As such, most of the delay in implementing infrastructural developments could have been more as a result of loan protocols than corruption.

Postwar Sierra Leone reproduces an economic geography reflecting that of the global political economy.[2] The regions in postwar Sierra Leone responsible for about three-quarters of the country's GDP receive lower, and fewer, public services than the capital city, which could be described as the domestic core (Government of Sierra Leone 2007). The lack of public services in the provincial areas of postwar Sierra Leone is partly a result of shortage in the national budget for public investment in infrastructure and social services. This not only results in the uneven distribution of public infrastructure and social services, it also creates spatial inequality traps, leaving much of Sierra Leone in a dire state of disrepair (Jalan and Ravallian 1997). In postwar Sierra Leone, only 8 percent of roads are paved (eStandardsForum 2009), as road maintenance only attract less than 1 percent of the Ministry of Works' annual budget. Similarly, total health expenditure makes up only 3.5 percent of the country's GDP (World Health Organization 2008).

When there are such budgetary constraints in postwar Sierra Leone, vulnerable groups such as women and children, particularly in the rural areas, bear the brunt of the resulting inequality (IMF 2005; Amnesty International 2009). Rural infrastructure is either nonexistent or substandard. It is therefore not surprising that vulnerable people in rural postwar Sierra Leone suffer higher rates of poverty, death, illiteracy, and hunger. In 2004, while over 70 percent of Sierra Leoneans lived below the poverty line (IMF 2005), only 15 percent of those live in Freetown, the capital of Sierra Leone. Seventy-nine percent of that number lived in the rural or urban areas outside the capital (World Bank 2008; IMF 2005). Average life expectancy is forty years; probability of dying before age five is 269:1, and average healthy life expectancy is about thirty-eight years.

Access to healthcare is limited to about 40 percent of Sierra Leone's population, with an estimated 0.5 percent contact between people and health facilities. In addition, about 56 percent of Sierra Leoneans surveyed in 2005 use the "nonofficial sector"[3] of the health system or do not seek healthcare at all (Médecines San Frontières 2006). Only 23 percent of the poor seek medical care when they need it (Government of Sierra Leone 2005, 38). The healthcare system, as presently constituted, creates health inequalities, as there are no protection mechanisms for the poor and the most vulnerable in terms of their ability to access the system (Amnesty International 2009). The institution of a cost-recovery, or user-fee program, which started with the IMF conditionalities on Sierra Leone, has prevented the poor and most vulnerable from accessing the health care system (Médecines San Frontières 2006; Amnesty International 2009). In addition, maternal health care has become precarious, with one in eight women in postwar Sierra Leone dying at childbirth (Amnesty International 2009).

The education sector is probably second only to health in terms of disruption and inequality. Over 60 percent of Sierra Leoneans are illiterate. Freetown has twice the amount of literacy than any other region in the country (World Bank 2007, 24). This is not surprising, as 60 percent of the government's expenditure is focused on Freetown and other urban areas. Total government expenditure, as a percent of GDP, increased from 2.9 percent in 1999 to 7.9 percent in 2005. The government consistently increased expenditure by about 11 percent between 1999 and 2005, with projections of a drop to about 3 percent in 2008 (Wang 2007, 96–100).

Notwithstanding the increase in the expenditure for education and the progress made in building more schools and enrolling more children in schools, many children still do not go to school, and the vast majority of them are from the rural areas outside the capital city Freetown. Gender disparities in education become pronounced at the secondary and tertiary levels, although socioeconomic and geographic disparities are greater (Wang 2007). A male student consumes 30 percent more in education expenditures than a female student, whereas a student from an urban area consumes over twice the amount of resources consumed by a student from a rural area (Wang 2007, 131).

The attempt to integrate postwar Sierra Leone into the global market, coupled with pressures from international financial institutions and powerful nations to liberalize economic policies and open their markets, have also contributed to the inequalities discussed above. The tenets of economic liberalization policies require the government of Sierra Leone to reduce its work force, cut government expenditure, and privatize government-owned industries and companies, while at the same time requires intensifying their revenue collection (Jubilee USA 2008). President Ernest Koroma, in his address to parliament, declared that "those [government workers] who do not add 'value' to service will be retrenched" (Government of Sierra Leone 2009b). The privatization of government-owned enterprises[4] and retrenchment of low-level civil servants has added to the ranks of the unemployed. This could translate into government unpopularity.

To ameliorate government unpopularity, successive governments have, in many cases, retrenched those workers who they perceive as opposition supporters or those from certain regions of the country.

Governments in postwar Sierra Leone have exploited such dire situations by resorting to neopatrimonialism in order to strengthen their political position. For instance, during the global scarcity of rice, and the corresponding increase in prices in early 2008, Sylvanus Koroma, the brother of President Koroma, was given duty-free concessions to import rice so that he could not only sell it cheaper, but also use it as a tool to strengthen the president's neopatrimonial ambitions by selling it to known supporters of the government (*Patriotic Vanguard* 2008; *Awareness Times* 2009a).

In addition, foreign assistance and policy reform for agriculture have also been used to bolster political patronage by the government. Tractors donated by countries like Libya to enhance food security policy reform were all sent to the northern part of Sierra Leone in 2008. Northern Sierra Leone is considered the stronghold of the current All Peoples' Congress (APC) government led by President Ernest Koroma (*Tripoli Post* 2008; *Awareness Times* 2009b). Such phenomena do not only exacerbate inequality, they also suggest discrimination vis-à-vis other regions of the country. These actions also breed national divide and animosity, particularly on the part of those regions of Sierra Leone that may feel left out of national development.

Government jobs, military promotions, and cabinet positions have also been used as tools for maintaining support by rewarding known or professed supporters of the APC government with lucrative jobs, sometimes irrespective of qualification or fitness for such jobs (International Crisis Group 2008). The military also has not been spared from such neopatrimonial meddling by the government of President Ernest Koroma. Seventy-five percent of the brigade and battalion commanders of the Sierra Leone military are from the northern region, which is the region of origin of President Koroma (*Global Times Online* 2009). Similar claims have been made concerning regional and tribal imbalance and favoritism when it comes to promotion into the officers' corps, wherein about 80 percent of those commissioned as officers were from President Koroma's Limba ethnic group (*New Vision* 2009). Such patterns of promotion in the military is diametrically opposed to Article XVII, subsection three, of the Lomé Peace Accord, which states that "recruitment into the armed forces shall reflect the geo-political structure of Sierra Leone within the established strength."

Reports (i.e., International Crisis Group 2008) have indicated that Sierra Leoneans from the southern and eastern regions of Sierra Leone have lost their jobs because of their regions of origin and/or their perceived political leanings. The cabinet of president Koroma is regionally biased, with fifteen of the twenty-two-member cabinet and sixteen of the twenty-two deputy ministers from the north of Sierra Leone (Government of Sierra Leone 2009a; International Crisis Group 2008). The same is true for state-owned enterprises, where twelve of the sixteen chairs of the various boards are from the north. It should be noted that the cabinet and appointments to state-owned enterprises of the previous government of Ahmed Tejan-Kabbah were relatively more balanced on the basis of region and ethnicity. For instance, Tejan-Kabbah's government was comprised of eight cabinet ministers chosen from the north, seven from the south, four from the east, and three from the west. The International Crisis Group, a nongovernmental organization dedicated to advising governments on the prevention and resolution of deadly conflicts, reported that the government of Ernest Koroma had "exacerbated regional political rivalries by dismissing numerous functionaries appointed by the previous administration and replacing them with APC-supporting northerners" (International Crisis Group 2008, i). The departure from the vision of inclusiveness, which was integral in not only the Lomé Peace Accord, but also in previous peace agreements, and the embrace of an unwritten policy of exclusion, on the one hand, and the use of government jobs to placate clients, on the other, by the government of President Koroma suggests that the government has already forgotten some of the reasons for the outbreak of the war.

"Neopopulism" is also on the rise in postwar Sierra Leone. Unorganized and unemployed urban youth are becoming increasingly important in these neopopulist strategies. The ruling APC party maintains a task force comprised of unemployed youth and ex-combatants whose role is, most times, to spread fear among the populace through intimidation and violence. The remobilization of ex-combatants actually started in 2006 during the run up to the 2007 presidential elections (Christensen and Utas 2008). The youth are promised a stake in pro-poverty programs through a proposed youth commission that could be used by the leadership to recruit and build support. The use of unemployed youth by the political elite as cannon fodder in their competition for control of government is not only of neopatrimonial character, but it could also facilitate a rapid resurgence of a culture of violence in politics.

Elite Control

Implications for Postwar Sierra Leone

The implications of the reproduction of global inequalities for postwar Sierra Leone cannot be over emphasized. The Lomé Peace Accord was meant to address the many inequalities that existed before, and informed the brutality of, the war. While the accord was signed between the RUF and the government of Sierra Leone, its provisions are guidelines for the maintenance of postwar peace by subsequent governments of Sierra Leone. That the inequalities are not only persistent but seem to be perpetuated by the government of Ernest Koroma suggests either an act of ignoring the Lomé accord or dismissing the dangers of the possible breakdown of the tenuous and fragile negative peace in Sierra Leone.

Using government jobs to reward party loyalists, and using regional origin as a criterion for promotion in the civil service and the military, is a recipe for disaster in Sierra Leone. Such actions do not only deepen inequalities of income, they also deepen ethnic divide in the country. Some of the grievance of the coup plotters in 1992 and 1997 included tribalism and nepotism in government-hiring practices (Gberie 2005; Sierra Leone Web 1997). Specifically, Johnny Paul Koroma, the leader of the brutal AFRC junta, cited the failure on the part of the government of Ahmed Tejan-Kabbah to implement the Abidjan Peace Accord, which included ethnic balance both in the military and government appointments as justification for his coup (Gberie 2005).

The continued exclusion of other citizens from attaining certain positions in the government and the military due to their ethnicity, region of origin, or perceived political leanings does not only take away their rights as citizens and marginalize them as a group, it could lead also to deep-seated resentment for the government. The implication here is that the APC government, through its actions, is recultivating regional and ethnic grievance. When a people realizes that winning elections and controlling government is the surest way to access jobs for which they are otherwise qualified, they would either join the party in power or seek other means, which are not necessarily legitimate, to take control of the government. On the other hand, those in the government realizing their actions of discrimination and marginalization of other Sierra Leoneans could also ensure (mostly by undemocratic means) that they hold on to power by any means necessary. The creation of such an atmosphere could easily lead to an outbreak of violence and a possible return to civil war.

Conclusion

Global inequalities continue to affect the ability of postwar Sierra Leone to address the internal structural violence it faces, making the recurrence of another conflict likely. Minimizing structural violence and achieving positive peace in Sierra Leone requires meaningful democratization of the global structures perpetuating inequalities, particularly in the realm of international trade, finance, and development. Cosmopolitan actions through organizations like the UN and other nongovernmental organizations have succeeded, to some extent, in getting international financial institutions to review their modus operandi in order to make it more friendly and cognizant of the realities of poor countries like Sierra Leone. Rich, industrialized nations must realize that a prosperous third world would be to their advantage (Gilpin 2001). As such, it will make sense for them to use their bully pulpit to institute trade, finance, and development regimes that are not biased toward their hegemonic interests. Constantly keeping poor countries like Sierra Leone in a dependency mode would only increase internal inequalities, which in turn may lead to conflict.

In the same vein, Sierra Leone must revisit its priorities and strive to minimize structural violence and other inequalities. The troubling resurgence of a culture of violence among the youth must be tackled with all urgency. The use of unemployed youth and ex-combatants for political intimidation must end. Also, all sectors of the country, particularly ethnic groups, must be made to feel as part of the governance apparatus. This will help minimize disgruntlement and possible conflict. The government of Sierra Leone must endeavor to institute a culture of meritocracy wherein government jobs and military promotions are based largely on merit instead of the perceived regionalism and political orientation.

Finally, the government of Sierra Leone must find ways to wean itself from global-aid economy. Unless the government of Sierra Leone can find ways to raise its own funds for the provision of social services, internal inequalities will continue to grow. As such, the government must focus on real policies devoid of populism, cronyism, and tribalism. Minimizing these vices of structural violence will go a long way in achieving relative positive peace in postwar Sierra Leone.

Notes

1. Structural violence refers to any constraint on human potential attributable to economic and political structures.
2. The global economic geography is divided into a global division of labor, with the core embarking on capital-intensive production, the semi-periphery having both capital -and labor-intensive production, and the periphery relegated to labor-intensive production.
3. The "nonofficial sector" includes traditional healers, unauthorized ambulatory pharmacists (unauthorized ambulatory pharmacists are known as *pepe* doctors), home visits by nurses, and other alternatives.
4. Privatization of government-owned enterprises is subsequently followed by streamlining the work force by laying off workers.

References

Abdullah, Ibrahim. 1998. Bush path to destruction: The origin and character of the Revolutionary United Front/Sierra Leone. *Journal of Modern African Studies* 36 (2): 203–35.

American Political Science Association. 2008. Report of the task force on difference, inequality and developing societies. Washington, DC: American Political Science Association.

Amnesty International. 2009. Out of reach: The cost of maternal health in Sierra Leone. http://www.amnesty.org/en/library/asset/AFR51/005/2009/en/9ed4ed6f-557f-4256-989f-485733f9addf/afr510052009eng.pdf.

Awareness Times. 2009a. SLPP Blasts APC Corruption over 1 Million Dollars Waiver to President's Brother. April 9. http://www.news.sl/drwebsite/publish/article_200511793.shtml.

———. 2009b. Libyan green program supports Sierra Leone food security. April 24. http://www.news.sl/drwebsite/publish/article_200511967.shtml, retrieved October 3, 2009.

Chege, Michael. 2002. Sierra Leone: The state that came back from the dead. *The Washington Quarterly* 25 (3): 147–60.

Christensen, Maya, and Mats Utas. 2008. Mercenaries of democracy: The "politricks" of remobilized combatants in the 2007 general elections, Sierra Leone. *African Affairs* 107 (429): 515–39. http://afraf.oxfordjournals.org/cgi/content/abstract/107/429/515.

Conteh-Morgan, Earl. 2004. Peace building and human security: A constructivist perspective. Paper presented at the Conference of Peace Building and Human Security, Hiroshima, Tokyo.

Dreher, Axel, and Nathan Jensen. 2007. Independent actor or agent? Empirical analysis of the impact of the U.S. interests and International Monetary Fund conditions. *Journal of Law and Economics* 50 (1): 105–124.

eStandardsForum. 2009. Country Briefs: Sierra Leone. Financial Standards Foundation, December 11. *http://www.estandardsforum.org/system/briefs/315/original/brief-Sierra%20Leone.pdf?1265906888*

Gberie, Lansana. 2005. *A dirty war: The RUF and the destruction of Sierra Leone.* Bloomington: Indiana University Press.

Gilpin, Robert. 2001. *Global political economy: Understanding the international economic order.* Princeton, NJ: Princeton University Press.

Global Times Online. 2009. Regionalism rocks army promotions. September 9. http://www.globaltimes-sl.org/news150.html.

Grant, J. Andrew. 2005. Diamonds, foreign AID and the uncertain prospects for post-conflict reconstruction in Sierra Leone. *The Round Table* 94 (381): 443–57.

Goldin, Ian, and Kenneth Reinert 2006. *Globalization for development: Trade, finance, AID, migration and Policy.* Washington, DC: World Bank.

Government of Sierra Leone. 2005. Poverty reduction strategy paper: A national program for food security, job creation and good governance 2005–2007. Freetown: *Sierra Leone Ministry of Finance.*

————. 2007. *Budget speech* delivered to the House of Parliament by Minister of Finance, John Benjamin. http://www.bankofsierraleone-centralbank.org/pdf/ Gov_Budget.pdf.

————. 2009a. Cabinet reshuffle. Press Release. *Office of the President*, Freetown, Sierra Leone, February 28. http://www.ernestkoroma.org/cabinet.htm.

————. 2009b. Presidential address to the third session of parliament, Freetown, Sierra Leone, October 9.

IAHM. 2005. IAHM startup project: Report module 2. International Association for Humanitarian Medicine. http://www.iahm.org/doc/sierra%20leone%20en .pub.pdf.

International Crisis Group. 2008. Sierra Leone: A new era of reforms? *International Crisis Group Africa Report*, No. 143, July 31.

International Monetary Fund. 2005. Sierra Leone: Poverty reduction strategy paper preparation status report. http://www.imf.org/external/pubs/ft/scr/2005/ cr05201.pdf.

Jalan, Jyotsna, and M. Ravallian. 1997. Spatial poverty traps? *World Bank Policy Research Policy Paper Series 1982*. Washington, DC: World Bank.

Jubilee USA. 2008. Are IMF and World Bank economic policy conditions undermining the impact of debt cancellation? Briefing Note Three. Washington, DC: Jubilee USA.

Kandeh, Jimmy. 1999. Ransoming the state: Elite origins of subaltern terror in Sierra Leone. *Review of African Political Economy* 26 (81): 349–66.

Keen, David. 2005. *Conflict and collusion in Sierra Leone*. New York: Palgrave.

Lamin, Abdul Rahman. 2003. Building peace through accountability in Sierra Leone: The Truth and Reconciliation Commission and the special court. *Journal of Asian and African Studies* 38 (2–3): 295–320.

Médecine sans Frontières. 2006. Access to healthcare in postwar Sierra Leone. *Summary of 2005 Survey of Four Districts: Kambia, Tonkolili, Bombali, Bo*. Amsterdam: Médecine Sans Frontières.

McIntyre, Angela, and Thokozani Thusi. 2003. Children and youth in Sierra Leone's peace building process. *African Security Review* 12 (2): 73–80.

Murshed, S. Manshoob. 2005. Inequality, indivisibility and insecurity. Paper presented at the UNU/WIDER Jubilee Conference, June 17–18, Helsinki, Finland. http://mrgec.mcgill.ca/Papers/murshed,%20feb%2005.pdf (accessed October 10, 2007).

New Vision. 2008. Danger: Tribalism rocks Salone army. September 9. http:// newvisionnews.com/index.php?option=com_content&task=view&id=474&Ite mid=1.

Patriotic Vanguard. 2008. Rice prices down. July 31. http://www.thepatriotic vanguard.com/spip.php?article2911.

Prasad, Eswar, Kenneth Rogoff, Shang-Jin Wei, and M. Ayhan Kose. 2004. Effects of financial globalization on developing countries: Some empirical evidence. *IMF Occasional Paper 220*. Washington, DC: International Monetary Fund.

Polaski, Sandra. 2006. *Winners and losers: Impact of the Doha round on developing countries*. Washington, DC: Carnegie Foundation.

Ramsbotham, Oliver, Tom Woodhouse, and Hugh Miall. 2005. *Contemporary Conflict Resolution*. 2nd ed. Cambridge: Polity.

Rashid, Ishmael. 2004. Student radicals, lumpen youth and the origins of revolutionary groups in Sierra Leone. In *Between Democracy and Terror: The Sierra Leone Civil War*, ed. Ibrahim Abdullah, 66–89. Pretoria: University of South Africa Press.

Rippon, Thomas J., and Stan Willow. 2004. Sierra Leone: A model for a program for action for a culture of peace. *OJPCR: The Online Journal of Peace and Conflict Resolution* 6 (1): 152–69.

Richards, Paul. 1996. *Fighting for the rain forest*. London: Oxford University Press.

Riddell, Barry. 2005 Sierra Leone: Urban-elite bias, atrocity and debt. *Review of African Political Economy* 32 (103): 115–33.

Sierra Leone Web. 1997. Address by Major Johnny Paul Koroma. May 27. http://www.sierra-leone.org/AFRC-RUF/AFRC-052897.html.

Stiglitz, Joseph E. 2003. *Globalization and its discontents*. New York: W. W. Norton.

Statistics Sierra Leone. 2008. *Annual Statistical Digest 2005/2006*. Statistics Sierra Leone, Freetown. http://www.statistics.sl/FINAL%20DIGEST%202006.pdf.

Strange, Susan. 1983. Cave! Hic Dragones: A critique of regime analysis. In *International Regimes*, ed. Stephen D. Krasner, 337–54. Ithaca, NY: Cornell University Press.

Tripoli Post. 2008. Libya donates tractors to Sierra Leone. September 21. http://tripolipost.com/articledetail.asp?c=1&i=2379.

United Nations Development Program. 2005. *Human Development Report*. New York: UNDP.

———. 2009. *Human Development Report*. New York: UNDP.

Wallerstein, I. 1998. The present state of the debate on world inequality. In *Development and Underdevelopment: The Political economy of global inequality*, ed. M. A. Seligson and J. T. Passe-Smith, 277–90. Boulder, CO: Lynne Rienner.

Wang, L. 2007. *Education in Sierra Leone: Present challenges, future opportunities*. Washington, DC: World Bank Publications.

Washington Post. 2008. A mother's final look at life. November 12. http://www.washingtonpost.com/wp-dyn/content/article/2008/10/11/AR2008101102165.html.

World Health Organization. 2008. *World Health Statistics 2008*. Geneva, Switzerland: World Health Organization.

Zack-Williams, A. B. 1999. Sierra Leone: The political economy of civil war, 1991–1998. *Third World Quarterly* 20 (1): 143–62.

Afterword

The Future of Sierra Leone

Dick Simpson

A consensus political history of Sierra Leone during the last fifty years since independence is beginning to emerge from the views of both scholars and participants.[1]

When British colonialism ended and the nation gained its independence in 1961, it was a time a great hope. Under both Sir Milton and Albert Margai as the first prime ministers, a positive future of economic development and political democracy was foreseen. After all, the British left behind a functioning road and rail system, a relatively capable civil service, and a working public school system. However, achieving independence had been speeded by international events of the 1960s, so there was not a smooth a transition to the nation. Yet there was a two-party system, a parliament, and successful elections. Equally important, the country was self-sufficient in food production, such as rice, although luxury foods were imported. The country had an abundance of diamonds and other mineral wealth beyond that of neighboring states. Particularly with its Krio population, it had an educated class, and in Fourah Bay College, it had the best university in British West Africa.

When I spent 1966 in the country, I concluded that with its party system and its local, town, chiefdom, and district government councils, Sierra Leone was on the path to economic development and political democracy.

My Graduate Assistant at the University of Illinois at Chicago, Tom Kelly, provided valuable assistance in creating early drafts of this chapter and in doing the statistical analysis of the public opinion data provided by The Centre for Development and Security Analysis under Professor Osman Gbla, Dean of Social Sciences and Law at Fourah Bay College in Sierra Leone.

It was not to be. With a military coup annulling the results of the 1967 elections, a downward spiral began that has included five military coups and a terrible eleven-year civil war that nearly destroyed the nation.

Despite the All Peoples' Congress (APC) winning the national election, Siaka Stevens was exiled by the military coup of 1967. When Stevens was reinstated as prime minister by the third military coup, he moved the country, step by step, to dictatorial control under his presidency, in what became a one-party state. Elections were dominated by political thuggery afterwards.

There were a number of problems in concentrating all of the power in President Stevens and the APC. Other power centers were systematically destroyed so that they could not challenge the ruling party or the president. Local councils were suspended and the government took over the appointment of paramount chiefs, rendering many of them illegitimate in the eyes of the people. The parliament was emasculated into a rubber stamp for the president. The Sierra Leone People's Party (SLPP), which ruled the country from 1961 to 1967, was made illegal, and was therefore unable to hold the government accountable or to provide alternative policies. Many cabinet ministers were incompetent, out only for their own profit through graft and corruption. All major decisions and projects had to be personally approved by President Stevens, which created a bottleneck in making any decisions.

Like most African nations, Sierra Leone's economy worsened in the 1970s and 1980s. This made it impossible to provide for a better life for its nearly six million citizens. Stevens and his successors were kept in power by use of corruption and favoritism in order to reward the political and business elite, especially leaders of the APC and businessmen involved in illegally trading diamonds. Civil servants and teachers often went without their salaries, and electricity, roads, and infrastructure deteriorated. The railway, instead of being modernized, was destroyed.

All of these problems were compounded by spectacularly bad decisions, such as President Stevens's prideful choice to host the Organization of African Unity (OAU) meeting in Freetown in 1980 at the ruinous cost of millions of U.S. dollars.

When Siaka Stevens passed the presidency to his successor, Major-General Joseph Momoh, in 1985, the country went from bad to worse. Siaka Stevens was decisive, even if he ruled with an iron fist. President Momoh was indecisive and incompetent to govern. Corruption flourished at ever-greater levels. The economic suffering of the people only increased. At the same time, diamond and other mineral wealth continued to be plundered.

Thus, when the Revolutionary United Front (RUF) began the "revolution" in the eastern region of Sierra Leone in 1991, many Sierra Leoneans were prepared to support it, including civil servants in Freetown, upcountry farmers, and local people in the countryside. Unfortunately, what was unleashed was not a true revolution or even a civil war in the usual sense. Instead, it was anarchy, a war of all against all, and a manifestation of evil as described in Joseph Conrad's *Heart of Darkness.*

Because of the war, one-third of Sierra Leoneans had to flee their homes. Even the capital, Freetown, was sacked twice. More than fifty thousand Sierra Leoneans died, and several thousands had limbs amputated by child soldiers. The Sierra Leonean Army was as vicious and irresponsible as the rebels. The civil war was finally ended in 2002, only by the intervention of Economic Community of West African States Monitoring Group (ECO MOG) troops under Nigerian leadership and, eventually, the direct-armed intervention by Britain.

After the intervention of the British, Sierra Leone, with the support of the international community in the postwar period, has begun the rebuilding process. This book traces the post-Lomé record in disarmament, demobilization, and reintegration (DDR) of the combatants, the two successful national elections of 2002 and 2007, the reconstruction of destroyed infrastructure, and the development of NGOs and civil society. Since the end of the civil war, negative peace has been achieved, and steps toward a more positive peace have been taken. The historical question now is whether or not development and democracy can be achieved in current postwar conditions that include a drastic international economic recession.

Postwar Sierra Leone

Essays in this book have recounted both the problems and the positive gains since the Lomé Peace Accord was signed a decade ago. In the postwar rebuilding effort, Stevens's one-party state of "authoritative centralism" and unopposed elections have been replaced by multiparty elections in which the SLPP government was peacefully replaced by an APC national government in 2007. The local governments of district and town councils, which had been eliminated under President Stevens, have been reestablished. Successful local government elections were held in 2008. However, poverty, illiteracy, a weak economy, poor infrastructure, an inadequate education system, continuing abuses in tribal courts, and a high level of corruption remain.

Sierra Leone is not economically self-sufficient. Over 50 percent of government funds for various economic and social programs in the country, including the holding of elections, come from the international community's foreign aid—not from taxes paid by Sierra Leoneans. And while economic indicators have improved since the war, while real Gross Domestic Product (GDP) contracted by over 5 percent a year and inflation was over 33 percent annually, the numbers are still not as positive as they need to be. Average annual GDP growth since the war stands at 6.5 percent, but inflation has continued to outpace growth. Inflation has averaged 9.7 percent per year since the war and grew to 16.6 percent in 2008 (Korsu and Baima 2009, 6). The youth, who have crowded into the urban centers partially in the aftermath of the war, remain 70 percent unemployed. While the AIDS epidemic is not as terrible as in other African countries, it is still fierce, with at least 7 percent of the country infected. The general health system in the country is in shambles, contributing to one of the worst infant and child mortality rates in the world. Meanwhile, the population remains at least 60 percent illiterate, which means that until better education is provided, Sierra Leone will remain uncompetitive in the global economy.

Current Views of Sierra Leoneans

Despite its many problems, especially those related to recovery from the civil war, reestablishment of civil society, and rebuilding the country, the most recent public opinion polls demonstrate that Sierra Leoneans are still remarkably positive in their outlook. And as McCormack-Hale (this volume) indicated, they support democracy and development in principle.

The Centre for Development and Security Analysis (CEDSA) undertook a public opinion poll of college students in 2008. Adults in Freetown, Bo, Kenema, and Makeni were then surveyed in 2009. These polls revealed that 75 percent or more of college students and adults from all tribal groups, sections of the country, and political affiliations believe their lives, their families' lives, and their country will be better off in the next five years than they are today.

There are objective reasons for this optimism. The lives of most Sierra Leoneans have improved since the bloody civil war and the Lomé Peace Accord. The country is secure and the Sierra Leone Army today is better trained and controlled than before the war. Seventy-seven percent of all Sierra Leoneans say that the armed forces are doing a better job than they did before the war. In addition, the crime rate in Sierra Leone is actually lower than the average city in the United States. In a country in which no one was safe less than a decade ago, this is a major accomplishment.

Since it is still recovering from the bloody civil war, citizens' sense of safety and their views of the army and the police are particularly critical. When asked about their perceptions of Sierra Leone police, more than half (59 percent) of those interviewed by CEDSA responded that police were doing a better job than before the war. However, approval of the armed forces rated much higher, with nearly 80 percent saying the military was doing a better job. Perhaps most y, when asked if they felt safe in their own neighborhoods, more than ent of all Sierra Leoneans said they did.

Objectively, however, living conditions in Sierra Leone remain among the worst in the world. Two-thirds of the people live in absolute poverty, and more than one in four endure extreme poverty. Per capital income in 2006 was only US$228, *less than in the 1980s before the war*. Most of the people remain illiterate and lack clean water and sanitation. The infrastructure of the country has not improved sufficiently. Less than 7 percent of the country has adequate electricity. In urban areas, 84 percent of the people have water that is safe to drink, but only 64 percent of them have adequate and safe disposal of waste and sewage. In the rural areas, the levels of safe water and sanitation are only 32 percent and 17 percent (Bangura 2009).

As Victor Davies (this volume) points out, and as many observers of postwar Sierra Leone confirm, political corruption continues to be a major problem. In 2007, the country still ranked 150th out of 180 on the Transparency International perception index. In short, Sierra Leone is one of the most politically corrupt countries in the world. Schools do not get the government dispersed subsidies, hospitals do not get essential drugs, and civil servants still receive low salaries while corrupt officials steal the nation's wealth. National anticorruption laws have been enacted and the Anti-Corruption Commission has prosecuted, and continues to prosecute, public servants and government ministers. In spite of this, the commission is thus far seen as ineffective by most Sierra Leoneans.

Despite all these problems, most people in Sierra Leone report being satisfied with the direction of their country and the prospect for a better life for themselves, their families, and a positive future for the nation. When asked how their families and the country were doing compared to five years ago, about 60 percent of those surveyed by CEDSA concluded that they were doing better. About three-fourths believe that their families and the country will be doing better still five years from now.

More than two-thirds of both the college students and adults surveyed by CEDSA approved of the job that the Sierra Leonean national government was doing. Given the change in national government and the political controversies in the country, this is a very positive approval rating. However, the evaluations of the parliament elected in 2007 were lower than the approval of the national government in general. Less than 60 percent of those surveyed approved of the job the parliament was doing. And there were predictable splits among different ethnic groups. Among Temne adults, who are predominantly APC supporters, 70 percent thought the parliament was doing a good or excellent job, but only 46 percent of Mende adults, who are predominantly SLPP and PMDC supporters, had a positive view. Evaluations for their own specific members of parliament were lower than for parliament as a whole, with only slightly more than half of the constituents approving the job their own MPs are doing. This differs from many surveys in other nations in which the evaluations of the legislative branch are low, but individual legislators are rated highly because of their ability to deliver services to their constituents. MPs in Sierra Leone are not able to deliver significant public works, government jobs, or contracts because the national government funding is so limited that MPs themselves are underpaid and have insufficient funds for offices, equipment, and staff.

The majority of all respondents (79 percent) were happy with the results of local elections in July 2008. This was true among all party affiliations, although support from the APC was slightly higher than from the SLPP or PMDC supporters. Supporters of the minority NDA party reported being happy with the elections at the highest rate of 94 percent. Of those who supported the governing APC party, 80 percent believed their new local government would either do an excellent or a good job. Although significantly less optimism was expressed by SLPP supporters, almost two-thirds were happy with local elections, and a very strong majority thought that the new local governments would do well. This is an auspicious beginning for the newly elected governments.

Peacebuilding

The Lomé accord attempted to end the war and assure the sovereignty of Sierra Leone once again. Now that peace has finally come, the broader peacebuilding effort requires tackling the hard problems that helped to cause the war in the first place. While some ex-combatants have participated in job and skills training programs, most of those who did still found it difficult to gain employment. The funds for reintegration into society have been too little to alleviate unemployment. And the reparations for war victims promised by the Truth and Reconciliation Commission have yet to be delivered.

The Truth and Reconciliation Commission has issued its findings, elections have been held, local government reestablished, and new national laws have been enacted. But that is not enough, as existential and physical insecurities still loom large (Conteh-Morgan, Mustapha, this volume). The ruling APC maintains a "task force" of unemployed youth and ex-combatants to intimidate the public, particularly at election time. In addition, the cabinet of President Ernest Koroma does not fully represent all ethnic groups (Mustapha, this volume) and political factions, so ethnic tensions remain that may be exploited by politicians in the future to further divide the country and to undermine the legitimacy of the national government.

Public and Governmental Priorities

In the CEDSA public opinion poll, adults were given eight government priorities to rank in order of importance. An index was created to weigh the importance of each priority by giving points according to how it was ranked. A ranking of "1" yielded eight points, a ranking of "2" yielded seven points, and so on. The number of points was then divided by the number of respondents in order to create priority index score. The government functions ranked as most important by Sierra Leoneans, as measured by priority index scores, were as follows:

1. Education (6.65)
2. Health (5.79)
3. Security (4.97)
4. Agriculture (4.40)
5. Providing jobs for unemployed youth (4.01)
6. Development and road building (3.77)
7. Energy and Power (3.67)
8. Curbing Corruption (2.96)

These public priorities do not mirror the actual expenditures of the national government. National government expenditures for 2008 were Le 1,018,621,700,000 or US$339.5 million. The two largest expenditures were 35 percent spent on salaries and wages of national government employees and 16 percent to pay the interest on national and international public debts. The expenditures for different sectors in the budget are shown in Table A.1.

One of the several mismatches between the opinions about priorities among Sierra Leoneans and actual government expenditures is in

Table A.1   Sierra Leone budget allocations by category, 2008

Budget Categories	Percent of Budget
Salaries and wages	35%
Public debt	16%
Energy and power	8%
Security sector	7%
Development activities	6%
Road fund	5%
Education	5%
Health	3%
All other expenditures	15%

Total national budget Le 1,018,621,700,000 or US$339.5 million
Source: The Centre for Development and Security Analysis. 2008. Parliament Update. No. 2.

agriculture. Agriculture is seen by many as the backbone of the Sierra Leone economy, especially because it serves as main source of livelihood for about three-quarters of the population. However, the agricultural sector receives just about 1 percent of the national government's budget. (Because it is so small, it is lumped into the "other miscellaneous" category in Table A.1.) When the globe is experiencing food shortages and there is a government policy to guarantee food security in Sierra Leone, the country needs to be able to spend more to ensure food self-sufficiency and security. But the Sierra Leonean government does not have the revenue to do so. Therefore, it is almost entirely dependent on grants from international agencies and the market economy to improve its food production in order to move toward self-sufficiency and to bring in revenue from sales of agricultural products overseas.

Likewise, education, which is ranked as the most important function of government by the public, is only sixth in expenditures by the Sierra Leonean government. While both the government and international donors believe education is important, there is simply not enough money to support it. Foreign aid has assisted the government in building new schools, but not in paying teachers, providing books, and necessary school supplies, or in lowering school fees necessary to provide universal public education.

In the CEDSA survey, respondents were also asked about taxes, school fees, and prices in general. Almost three-fourths of the adults surveyed responded that taxes and school fees were too high, and more than four out of five believed that prices for goods and services were too high. However, when asked if they were willing to pay more in taxes if they believed that it would improve life in Sierra Leone, greater than three-fourths responded, "Yes."

There are some regional differences in the willingness to support higher taxes. In Makeni, 91 percent would do so. Even though Bo had the lowest percentage of those willing to pay more, still more than two-thirds of its residents said that they were willing to. One of the greatest challenges in such a poor country as Sierra Leone has been to establish taxes sufficient to run the government and to provide the necessary public services. However, in surveys, citizens indicate that they would be willing to pay taxes if they had greater faith in their government to use the money wisely. When they see rampant waste and corruption, they are less willing to support the government with their taxes. But in Freetown, the city government under Mayor Herbert George Williams has convinced businesses to begin to pay their fair share of taxes to local government. This is a hopeful sign.

Power and Corruption

In the CEDSA poll, a plurality of citizens (43 percent) viewed the government as less corrupt than before the war, but about a third of adults (32 percent) perceived more corruption now. When given four choices for the cause of corruption, 40 percent of adults chose "a lack of political will and corruption in high places." This seems to confirm a similar poll, the Sierra Leone Anti-Corruption Poll in 2000. However, when asked about the causes of corruption, 37 percent of college students placed the blame on "a lack of cooperation from the public in preventing corruption." In short, adults and college students believe corruption continues because of a lack of will on the part of the government and the public to curb it. And when it comes to corruption, almost 80 percent of adults believed that low pay is an important influence on the corruption by public officials. Until government corruption is curbed, no Sierra Leonean government is likely to have legitimacy in the eyes of its own people or in the international community.

Since independence in 1961, there has been a fundamental change in those perceived to have the most power—the leaders of the country. Those perceived to have power in Sierra Leone today are mostly government officials and politicians. Government administrators were chosen by almost one in three adults (31 percent) as being the most powerful in the country. Less than one in five (17 percent) chose elected officials as being the ones with power despite the formal legal structure of the nation. Politicians were chosen by another 12 percent, making a total of about six in ten adults choosing one of these groups.

Traditional chiefs and other traditional officials have clearly lost power in the eyes of the public, and even more so in the eyes of college students. In Freetown, only 18 percent believed traditional leaders had power, much lower than the other three provincial towns, where roughly one in three adults thought so. Traditional leaders were chosen as powerful by 28 percent of all adults. This is in stark contrast to only 9 percent of college students who shared this perception of traditional leaders as important. At the time of independence, traditional leaders, government administrators, and even educators were seen to be important leaders (Simpson1968). The power of government administrators and politicians has increased over the years since independence, while the power and influence of traditional officials has declined.

In terms of the key organizations in the country, the majority of adults (54 percent) did not approve of the jobs that political parties in general have been doing. Perceptions of parties in general varied from town to town. In Kenema, 54 percent approved of political parties, but only 37 percent did so in Bo. Political parties have yet to gain the trust of the population. Perhaps this is because of the role that political parties played in creating the dissatisfaction that led to the civil war. By contrast, non-governmental organizations (NGOs) were seen favorably by 87 percent of Sierra Leoneans. The media is also viewed positively, which is a hopeful sign. The performance of the media was rated as "excellent" or "good" by about three-fourths of all adults.

The Future

Since the Lomé Peace Accord was signed, "existential insecurity" still exists for many Sierra Leoneans. The war trials have been concluded. The lead prosecutor for the Special Court of Sierra Leone points out that these trials resulted in the first convictions for using child soldiers, the first convictions in world history for a "campaign of terror," the first convictions for sexual slavery, and the first convictions for "bush wives," that is, women who were conscripted into forced marriage (Rap 2009). The Truth and Reconciliation Commission established after the end of the war has issued its final report, although all its recommendations have yet to be carried out.

There has been disarmament and demobilization and improvements in some of the infrastructure that was destroyed by the war. Elections have been held successfully. New national and local governments have been established. Some institutions, like NGOs and the media, have broad public support. But reintegration of all the combatants has not been as successful and the economic disparities continue. Illiteracy and poverty, especially among the youth, are as prevalent as before the war. Public corruption continues to sap resources. Hopes for resurgence in agriculture, greater industrialization, and tourism have yet to be realized, although there are many public and private plans for a better future. The universities are up and running but face a shortage of books and funds for student scholarships.

A number of Sierra Leoneans in the diaspora that fled Sierra Leone either during the period of misrule or the civil war have begun to return. For instance, eighteen members of parliament are Sierra Leoneans who returned from their exile in the United States, and at least one member who returned from Britain won in the 2007 election. And those in the diaspora who remain abroad send very valuable foreign currency back to support families and friends in the transition from the war.

Sierra Leoneans, having experienced the terror of the civil war, vow that it will never happen again. While Sierra Leoneans recognize that they and their families are better off since the war and have a generally optimistic view about their and their country's future, the worldwide recession has only made development and a continuation of a positive and democratic peace more difficult. Inflation today is rampant again, with the Leone trading at about 3,500 Leones to a single U.S. dollar. There is a fear that "donor fatigue" will lessen international aid upon which the country still depends. Even if foreign aid continues, it is not at all clear that the priorities of foreign donors and international agencies mirror the priorities of the citizens of Sierra Leone or the requirements for rapid economic development. Simply adopting international standards in women's rights, environmental protection, children's rights, government accounting standards, and anti-corruption laws will not solve the fundamental problems of the country although they may be worthwhile in their own right.

The political parties still closely parallel the ethnic divisions of the country. The mineral wealth is still not exploited in a way to create maximum benefit for Sierra Leone and its impoverished people. While more land is being planted, progress in farming and the rural towns is slow. Even a provincial capital like Kenema is in many ways worse off today, especially with the fall in the sale of alluvial diamonds, than it was in the 1960s—the roads in town are in worse condition, for instance, and even the main road further into the interior is unpaved and nearly impassible.

The parliament remains a rubber stamp for the government, with inadequate staffing, pay, and facilities. Only six clerks are provided to handle all the parliamentary committees, and those committees are unable to provide the oversight function that they are supposed to play to insure that the national government is run efficiently. Members of parliament are still thought by the public as providing only patronage to their families and, perhaps, to some limited degree, to their constituents.

Local governments are in existence once again but many of the local government council members are ill equipped for their duties. The national government still sees these units of government as little more than additional administrative units to help collect taxes, to deliver minimal government services, and to keep the population docile. The traditional chiefdom governments have not adopted uniform laws, have tribal courts that frequently overtax and alienate the youth, and from the Siaka Stevens days, traditional chiefs are viewed as totally illegitimate in some chiefdoms. Integration of tribal and civil government remains a challenge for postwar Sierra Leone.

Despite all the challenges and difficulties, Sierra Leoneans still believe in a better future for themselves and their country. It remains to be seen if the post-Lomé and postwar years will be the beginning of the hopeful future that many thought would occur at the time of Independence fifty years ago.

Note

1. Joe A. D. Alie (1990) gives a more positive assessment of the regimes of Siaka Stevens and Joseph Momoh than most other accounts, although most of the factual material he uses is the same. Some of the other authors and historians that I consulted include Abdul Koroma (1996); Lansana Gberie (2005); Aminatta Forna (2002); Ismael Beah (2007); and Amadu Sesay (2007). I also interviewed a number of Sierra Leonean scholars, government officials, and former ministers under Stevens and Momoh in 2008 in developing this account.

References

Alie, Joe A. D. 1990. *A new history of Sierra Leone*. London: Macmillan.

Bangura, Sheka. 2009. The African peer review mechanism process Sierra Leone: A situational analysis of the country's socio-economic development. In *African Peer Review Mechanism-National Governing Council (APRM-NGC) report*. Freetown: African Peer Review Mechanism.

Beah, Ismael. 2007. *A long way gone*. New York: Farrar, Straus, and Giroux.

The Centre for Development and Security Analysis. 2008. *Parliament update*, no. 2. Freetown: Centre for Security and Development Analysis.

Forna, Amanita. 2002. *The devil that danced on the water*. New York: Atlantic Monthly Press.

Gberie, Lansana. 2005. *A dirty war in West Africa*. Bloomington: Indiana University Press.

Koroma, Abdul. 1996. *The agony of a nation*. Freetown: Andromeda Publications.

Korsu, Robert. D., and Samuel. J. Baima. 2009. The African peer review mechanism process Sierra Leone: Economic governance and management in Sierra Leone's APRM framework. In *African Peer Review Mechanism-National Governing Council (APRM-NGC) report*. Freetown: African Peer Review Mechanism.

Rap, Stephen. Interviewed on the program "Worldview." WBEZ Radio, February 2009. Chicago.

Sesay, Amadu. 2007. *Does one size fit all? The Sierra Leone Truth and Reconciliation Commission revisited*. Uppsala, Sweden: Nordiska Afrikaninstitueta.

Simpson, Dick. 1968. *The political evolution of two African towns: Kenema and Makeni, Sierra Leone*. PhD diss., Indiana University.

Contributors

Joseph Bangura holds a BA with honors in history from the University of Sierra Leone and MA and PhD degrees in history from Dalhousie University, Nova Scotia, Canada. Dr. Bangura is assistant professor of history and African studies and director of the African studies program at Kalamazoo College. His research interests include African intellectual and urban history, and state security and governance in sub-Saharan Africa. He has published works on social and political relations in colonial and postcolonial Sierra Leone and Islam in colonial Freetown.

Earl Conteh-Morgan is professor and director of graduate studies in the Department of Government and International Affairs at the University of South Florida. He is the author of, among other books, *Democratization in Africa: The Theory and Dynamics of Political Transitions* (Praeger, 1997); *Collective Political Violence—An Introduction to the Theories and Cases of Violent Conflicts* (Routledge, 2004); coauthored *Sierra Leone at the End of the Twentieth Century: History, Politics, and Society* (Peter Lang, 1999); and coedited *Peacekeeping in Africa: ECOMOG in Liberia* (St. Martin's, 1998). Dr. Conteh-Morgan has published on human security, conflict and peacebuilding, state failure, and the impact of globalization on state cohesion in refereed journals such as *Journal of Conflict Studies, Peace and Conflict Studies*, and *International Journal of Peace Studies*, among many others. Dr. Conteh-Morgan is currently researching Sino-African relations in the twenty-first century.

Victor A. B. Davies is with the African Development Bank. Mr. Davies' research interests span the economics of violent conflict, macroeconomic policy, and the political economy of economic growth and natural resources. He was the head of the Economics Department at Fourah Bay College, University of Sierra Leone, and a Visiting Scholar to the IMF Research Department. Mr. Davies has also served as a consultant to the World Bank and UNDP. He holds a doctoral degree in economics from the University of Oxford.

Doug Henry is an associate professor and medical anthropologist at the University of North Texas in Denton, Texas. He has published numerous articles on the Sierra Leone conflict, particularly in the areas of refugee health, continuing forms of "postconflict" violence, disasters and international aid, youth, and HIV.

Fredline M'Cormack-Hale is an assistant professor at the Whitehead School of Diplomacy and International Relations, Seton Hall University, where she teaches courses in international relations and African politics. She holds an MA and a PhD in political science from the University of Florida. Her research interests include gender, development, democratization, postconflict reconstruction and NGOs, with a focus on Sierra Leone.

Clarke Speed teaches in African studies and the University Honors Program at the University of Washington, Seattle. His interests include African religion, Landogo cosmology, the praxis of witchery and sorcery, apocalyptic collapse, secrecy, and the relationship of culture to violence.

Marda Mustapha is an assistant professor of political science at the College of Saint Rose in Albany, New York. He received his doctorate from Northern Arizona University, and his areas of expertise include global political economy, African politics, globalization, conflict, and democracy.

Susan Shepler is an assistant professor of international peace and conflict resolution in the School of International Service at American University in Washington, DC, where she teaches courses on youth and conflict, conflict in Africa, and qualitative research methods. She received a PhD in social and cultural studies in education from the University of California, Berkeley. She has done extensive ethnographic fieldwork in Sierra Leone with former child soldiers in interim care centers and in their communities after reintegration. Her dissertation *Conflicted Childhoods: Fighting Over Child Soldiers in Sierra Leone*, won the 2006 Gail Kelly Award from the Comparative and International Education Society for best dissertation in comparative education. She has also carried out research for UNICEF in Guinea on cross-border fosterage of children fleeing war, and for IRC on the long-term impact of teacher training for Liberian and Sierra Leonean refugees. She has participated in evaluations of peacebuilding programming for Search for Common Ground in Sierra Leone and Liberia. From 1987 to 1989, she taught secondary school in Sierra Leone as a Peace Corps Volunteer.

Dick Simpson is a University of Illinois at Chicago (UIC) professor and head of the department of political science. Professor Simpson is a specialist in city politics and elections. He came to UIC in 1967. He has won numerous teaching awards, such as the Silver Circle and UIC Excellence in Teaching Award. He is the author of sixteen books and over eighty professional articles and films.

Robert Tynes is an adjunct professor at SUNY New Paltz and SUNY Albany. He teaches comparative politics, international relations, and American foreign policy. His research interests include child soldiers, terrorism, and West Africa.

Alfred Zack-Williams is professor of sociology at the University of Central Lancashire and immediate past president of the African Studies Association of the United Kingdom, member of the British Academy Africa Panel, and member of the Editorial Working Group of the Review of African Political Economy. He is the author of *Tributors, Supporters and Merchant Capital: Mining and Underdevelopment in Sierra Leone* (Avebury, 1995), editor of *The Quest for Sustainable Development and Peace: The 2007 Sierra Leone Elections* (The Nordic African Institute, 2008), and coeditor, with I. E. Udogu, of *African Mosaic: Advancing the Political, Social, Health, Economic, Education and Information Communications Technology Issues in the Twenty-First Century* (Cambridge, 2009).

Index